Longman Keys to Language Teaching

Series Editor: Neville Grant

Techniques for Classroom Interaction

Donn Byrne

Pearson Educaiton Limited
Edinburgh Gate, Harlow,
Essex CM20 2JE, England
and Associated Companies throughout the world.

Published in the United States of America
by Longman Inc., New York

First published 1987
Reprinted 2001

BritishLibrary Cataloguing in Publication Data
Byrne, Donn, *1929-*
Techniques for classroom interaction.-
(Longman keys to language teaching)
1. Language and languages - Study and
teaching (Secondary)
I. Title
407'.12 P51
ISBN 0-582-74627-2

Library of Congress Cataloguing in Publicaiton Data
Byrne, Donn, 1929-
Techniques for classroom interaction.
(Longman keys to language teaching)
Includes index.
1. English language - Study and teaching - Foreign
speakers. 2. Interaction analysis in eduation.
3. Classroom management. I. Title. II. Series.
PE1128.A2B94 1987 428'.007 86-27579

Set in 10/12pt 'Monophoto' Century Schoolbook 227
Printed in China (EPC)

Contents

Preface

FOR SOME TIME, many teachers have felt the need for a series of handbooks designed for ordinary teachers in ordinary classrooms. So many books these days seem to be written for privileged teachers in privileged environments – teachers with large classrooms, large budgets for expensive equipment, and small classes!

However, most ordinary teachers are short of almost everything except students. These teachers don't have time for elaborate theories or complicated jargon.

Longman Keys to Language Teaching have been written especially for the ordinary teacher. The books offer sound, practical, down-to-earth advice on basic techniques and approaches in the classroom. Most of the suggested activities can be adapted and used for almost any class, by any teacher.

Techniques for Classroom Interaction is full of ideas on how to make our classrooms more active. Many students find it difficult to use the language to communicate. What activities can we bring in to help them – and how can we organise them? Should we always insist on accuracy – or are there times when we should encourage fluency and pretend not to notice the mistakes? Donn Byrne discusses such questions with his usual fund of practical advice and suggestions.

Neville Grant

What is classroom interaction?

Some classroom situations

Let's begin by looking at some typical classroom situations. As you will see both the teacher and the students are doing very different things in these situations. Can you see what the main differences are?

Classroom 1 Here the teacher is doing a drill.

T: ... John bought a shirt.
Cl: John bought a shirt.
T: Again!
Cl: John bought a shirt.
T: Good! Now ... a coat.
Cl: John bought a coat.
T: A pair of shoes.
Cl: John bought a pair of shoes. (etc.)

Classroom 2 Here the teacher is playing a language game with his students.

T: The other day I went shopping and I bought some new clothes. What did I buy? Try to find out! Ask me: Did you buy .....?
A: Did you buy a hat?
T: No, I didn't. I never wear a hat!
B: Did you buy a coat?
T: Yes, I did. A very nice one. But rather expensive!
C: Did you buy a shirt?
T: A shirt? Yes. In fact I bought three! (etc.) Now, all of you, write down three things *you* bought. ... Good! Are you ready? Let's go on. D, you start. Did you buy a pair of shoes?
D: No, I didn't.
E: Did you buy .....? (etc.)

Classroom 3 Here the teacher has written a short dialogue on the board.

> ***A: I went shopping last Saturday.***
>
> ***B: Oh? What did you buy?***
>
> ***A: Well, I bought a new coat.***
>
> ***B: Anything else?***
>
> ***A: Yes. I bought a pullover as well.***

The teacher has already got the class to practise the dialogue, first of all in chorus and then in pairs across the class and has already tried out some of the changes he or she wants the students to make (e.g. *the other day* and *yesterday* for *last Saturday*). The students now practise the dialogue on their own, in pairs.

Classroom 4 Here too the students are working in pairs. Each pair is writing a questionnaire, talking as they write. A and B's questionnaire begins like this:

> ***Name*** ....
>
> ***1 Are you interested in clothes?***
>
> ....
>
> ***2 What's your favourite colour?***
>
> ....
>
> ***3 What was the last thing you bought?***
>
> ....
>
> ***4 How much did you pay for it?***
>
> ....
>
> ***5 Are you wearing it now?***
>
> ....

After A and B have written their questionnaire, they each interview someone else in the class. Then they get together again to compare results.

Classroom 5 Here the teacher is having a discussion with the class.

T: Well, I sometimes get the impression ... I sometimes think ... that a lot of people today ... especially young people, I mean ... spend too much money on clothes. What do *you* think?
A: Oh, I don't think that's right. Maybe people buy more clothes, but they're quite cheap, really ...
B: ... and not very good, so ...
C: It depends. Anyway, clothes are important!
D: Yes.
T: Why, though?
C: Well, they ... show our ... personality ...
E: I don't agree. Most people buy something because, well, they see it in a shop ... or someone's wearing it, so they want it too ... (etc.)
T: Well, I suppose one good thing is ... making clothes provides work for people, doesn't it? (etc.)

Classroom 6 Here half a dozen students are sitting in a circle. They have been playing a game. During the game each student has won a sum of money. They are now telling each other how they will spend it.

A: How much did you win, B?
B: Me? £120.
C: Lucky! Well, what are you going to do with it?
D: She doesn't want to spend it. She doesn't like spending money!
B: Stop it! Well, first of all, I need some clothes ... (*All the students laugh*) ... so I'm going to buy a coat.
D: A new one?
B: Yes of course a new one. I'm going to spend half the money for that. And then ... (etc.)

Different kinds of interaction

As you can see, both the teacher and the students are doing very different things in these situations. It's not just the activities (drills, games, dialogue practice, etc.) that are different. Partly, it's the way the students are *organised* for work. Sometimes the teacher is working with the whole class together; sometimes the students are working in pairs or groups. And then there's the question of how much the teacher actually *controls* the class. Sometimes the students are free to say what they want; sometimes they are not. In fact, we have here six different kinds of classroom interaction. So let's look at these situations again in more detail to see what exactly is going on in each classroom. However, *before* you read on, why not look at the classroom situations again . . . and try to decide for yourself?

Classroom 1 Here the teacher is getting the students to repeat the same sentence pattern over and over again, with just a small change each time. The students don't have to *think* – because the teacher is putting the words into their mouths! On the other hand, they won't make any mistakes, unless they repeat something incorrectly.

The teacher is also working with the whole class together. He has decided that this is the best way of giving the students mass practice. So obviously he expects them to learn something in this way. Perhaps he is right; perhaps he is wrong. We will look at this question again later.

For the moment perhaps you'd like to ask yourself: how would *you* feel in this situation? You could be sure that – with the teacher controlling what you say – you are using *correct* language. But would you *enjoy* the activity?

Classroom 2 Again the teacher is working with the whole class, trying to get them to produce correct sentences (this time in the form of questions). He also wants to get a lot of repetition. But he has decided to use a language game instead of a drill. Why, do you think? Well, one reason must be that he hopes the students will find it more enjoyable.

Of course not everyone will get a chance to join in, especially in a large class. But most students will listen with attention, because they are interested. And afterwards the teacher can easily divide the students into pairs or groups, to carry on practising on their own.

Do you think *you* would enjoy this activity more than a drill? Why? Do you think that you would *learn* more this way?

Classroom 3 Here we have moved away from the whole class situation, although the teacher has done some whole class work first. The teacher wants to make sure that the students get a lot of *individual* practice. That's why he divides them into pairs, so that they can all practise at the same time. But he doesn't want them to make a lot of mistakes, so he has given them a model, in the form of a short dialogue. The students can introduce their own variations. They can even change the dialogue completely. The dialogue in itself isn't very exciting ... but, if you were an elementary student, would you enjoy using it to talk to a friend in the class, face to face? And wouldn't you like an opportunity to *say something in English*, without the teacher – and the rest of the class – listening?

Classroom 4 Again the students are working in pairs, but in a very different way. This time the teacher has given them a task: '*Write a questionnaire ...*'. He hasn't given them a model, but he has probably discussed some possible questions with them. But he isn't checking what they are saying and what they are writing. We hope that the students will check one another and, if they have any doubts, they can always ask the teacher.

As in Classroom 3, we don't know exactly what the teacher is doing at this stage. He may be helping one of the weaker students. He may even be writing a questionnaire himself because he wants to join in the activity!

This is very much a 'real-life' activity. Would you enjoy writing something which you could then use? And would you enjoy interviewing someone else in the class?

Classroom 5 Here the teacher is working with the whole class again. But he's talking with them in a very relaxed way – not at all like a teacher! He's also doing *some* of the talking – but not all of it. He wants to get the *students* to talk, to give *their* ideas, and he wants them to *keep on talking*. Of course, in a big class, they won't all get a chance to speak. But, if the discussion is reasonably interesting, they will probably all *listen* – especially if there is going to be a 'follow-up' activity.

What do you think the teacher's role in this discussion is? If you were giving *your* opinion in this discussion, would you want the teacher to listen to your ideas ... or correct your language?

Classroom 6 The students are on their own again, but this time they are working in groups. This is a good way of getting them to talk to one another. They have almost certainly enjoyed the game, but this follow-up activity – deciding what to do with the money they have won – should also prove quite enjoyable too. And it gives the game a kind of purpose. We don't know what kind of language the students will come out with. We hope they will use as much as they know – even if they make mistakes, as B does at the end.

We don't know what the teacher is doing while all this is going on. But if you were in one of the groups, talking about what you are going to do with the money you have won, would you want the teacher to interrupt and correct you if you made a mistake?

Some conclusions

Let's see what conclusions we can draw from our classroom situations. We will concentrate on three main points.

Whole class versus pairs or groups

First, whatever the size of your class (twenty, thirty, forty ... even sixty students) you can teach the whole class together or you can divide the students into pairs or groups. This is a very obvious point, but it is an important one, because you will continually have to make this decision. And you must know *why* you choose to do one or the other.

Teacher control

Secondly, you must decide whether you want – or need – to control what the learners are doing. If you teach the whole class together, it is easy (in a sense) to control everything. But you can do this in different ways. That is the difference between Classroom 1 and Classroom 2. But if you divide the students into pairs or groups, you can't expect to control the students to the same extent. But you can provide some control through the type of activity. That's the big difference between Classroom 3 and Classrooms 4 and 6.

What is your goal: accuracy or fluency?

Thirdly – and this is something we will keep coming back to – what is your main goal? For example, perhaps you want to make sure that the students get enough practice in a particular point of grammar or vocabulary or pronunciation. We will call this kind of work 'accuracy' activities: because their purpose is to make sure the students get something right. These activities usually form what is called the 'practice' stage of the lesson. If this is your aim, you will often want to work with the whole class, but you can use pair work (or even group work) for this purpose. Accuracy activities were being done in Classrooms 1, 2 and 3.

On the other hand, you may want to give your students opportunities to *use* the language they have learnt: to use it freely, even if they make mistakes. We will call this kind of work 'fluency' activities. They form what is often called the 'production' stage of the lesson. If this is your goal, you will usually want the students to work in groups (and sometimes in pairs). But because of the contribution you as the teacher can make, you may also want to do some fluency activities with the whole class. Fluency activities were being done in Classrooms 4, 5 and 6.

A model for classroom interaction

Two approaches

At the end of Chapter 1, we noted some key points. We can summarise and contrast them like this:

A	B
whole class teacher controlled accuracy activities	pairs and groups learner directed fluency activities

Of course, these key points do not always go together in this way, to form a kind of 'approach' to teaching. As we have already seen, you can use pair work for accuracy activities. On the whole, however, teachers often favour one approach or the other in their class work.

Approach A

For example, many teachers prefer to teach the whole class together, at least for most of the time. You can often hear these teachers say things like this:

I have to teach my students the language – grammar, vocabulary, pronunciation. They can't learn that in groups!

I've got too many students in the class. How could I do pairwork and groupwork? I couldn't control them!

I don't have enough time for things like pairwork and groupwork!

I need to be able to correct my students!

That is one point of view – a very common one, in fact. And teachers are right to make sure that their students learn 'the language' – particularly if they are going to be tested on this in the examination.

But we need to ask ourselves some questions. Is whole class work the *only* way of making sure that our students learn the language? Do we need to correct our students all the time? And is it really impossible to do pair work and group work if you have a very large class?

What do *you* think?

Approach B

What, then, about those teachers who take the opposite point of view? These teachers believe that students should spend most of their time working in pairs or groups because this is how they learn best – when they are interacting with one another. Of course the students will need preparation and guidance for this kind of work but, according to this approach, what they need most is *opportunities to use the language for themselves.*

You will often hear these teachers say things like this:

I still 'teach' my students. I just don't spend a lot of time working with the whole class, that's all.

My students learn because they really enjoy this kind of work.

My students don't need to spend a lot of time learning grammar.

If my students make mistakes, then I know what they need to learn!

Generally, teachers who take this point of view work in classrooms where they don't have many problems. Their classes are not too large and their students are well motivated – they *want* to learn. So they don't have to worry about discipline, about controlling their students, like many teachers with large classes.

Once again, however, we need to ask ourselves some questions. If students enjoy pair work and group work – and generally they do – won't this help them to learn? And don't students need opportunities to *use* language in the classroom – not just to practise grammar and vocabulary? If this is the case, can even teachers with large classes afford to neglect this approach?

What do *you* think?

A balanced approach

In practice, in most average teaching situations, we will probably need to use both these approaches: to give the students practice in grammar and vocabulary (accuracy work) and opportunities to use the language (fluency work) through a combination of class work, pair work and group work. But to do this effectively, we will need to organise our class work, pair work and group work so that the students really benefit from them, and to use a wide range of activities which will really motivate them. The model in the next section shows how we can begin to do this.

A model for classroom interaction

Let's look at the model itself first.

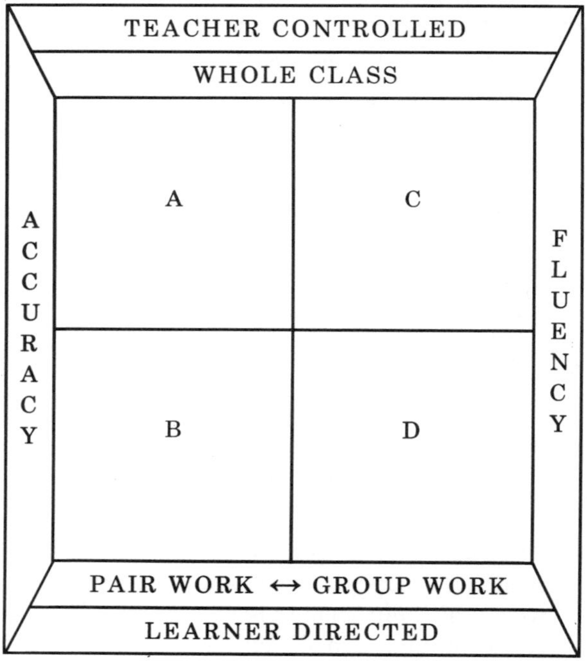

TEACHER CONTROLLED

WHOLE CLASS

ACCURACY

A C

B D

FLUENCY

PAIR WORK ↔ GROUP WORK

LEARNER DIRECTED

As you can see, there are four areas of interaction in the model. They are:

A *Accuracy activities* controlled by the teacher and done with the whole class.

B *Accuracy activities* directed by the learners and done in pairs (or occasionally in groups).

C *Fluency activities* controlled by the teacher and done with the whole class.

D *Fluency activities* directed by the learners and done in groups (or occasionally in pairs).

If you make use of these four different types of activity in your teaching, you can be reasonably sure that your students will get a balanced 'diet'. You can also be sure that both you and the learners will be making the best contribution to the lesson.

Some examples

Before we go any further, let's get some idea of the kind of activities you can do in each of these four areas. But once again, why not try to think of some for yourself *before* you read on?

Accuracy activities

Apart from drills, most traditional language games belong here. They are easy to do with the whole class (perhaps divided into teams, though) and they are usually intended to provide practice in specific bits of language. The guessing game in Classroom 2 belongs here. The teacher controls the activity because he wants to check what's going on.

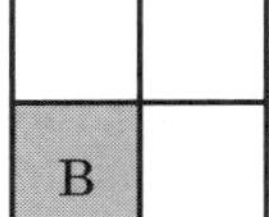

Mini-dialogue practice belongs here. The students work in pairs, using a model provided by the teacher, as in Classroom 3. The dialogue is intended to provide practice in grammar and vocabulary. The students can vary the dialogue or even go on to change it altogether.

Fluency activities

Our discussion activity in Classroom 5 belongs here. What is important is how the teacher interacts with the class or gets the students to interact with one another. If the teacher doesn't do this, the students should be doing the activity in groups.

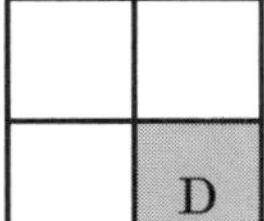

You can put here any activity which encourages the students to use language freely. For example, discussion, as we have just noted. Or playing the kind of game the students were doing in Classroom 6 – which produces 'talk' during and after the game.

Can *you* think of other activities for each of these four areas?

Some questions and answers

You will probably want to ask some questions at this point. Here are two possible ones.

How do I divide my time between accuracy and fluency work?

At an elementary level (let's say the first 100 or so hours of language learning), you will probably want to spend more time on accuracy work (A and B), in order to build up the learners' knowledge of grammar and vocabulary as quickly as possible. In this case, your class work will look something like this:

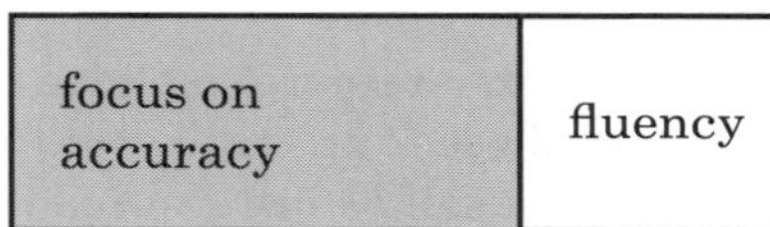

At an intermediate or advanced level, on the other hand, you will be able to spend much more time on fluency work. So your class work will look something like this:

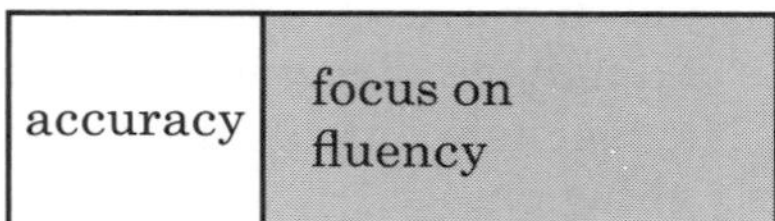

In what order do I do these activities?

The model doesn't really answer this question! It isn't intended to. It is a 'menu' rather than a 'recipe' for lesson planning. In the end, *you* must decide, taking into account your teaching situation and the level at which you are working. At an elementary level, for example, and working with a large class, you can safely follow the order of the activities in the model.

A → B → C / D

That is, you will generally need to start with some class work and pair work (for accuracy practice) before going on to do some kind of fluency work.

On the other hand, at an intermediate or advanced level, you should be able to move from fluency to accuracy work. That is, after the students have had a go at using the language, you can decide what they need to learn – or relearn.

Teacher roles

Although you are a teacher, you can't just say that your job is to 'teach'! Like an actor, you will have to play different roles at different times. The model can help you understand the different roles you will have to perform – depending on the kind of activity the students are doing.

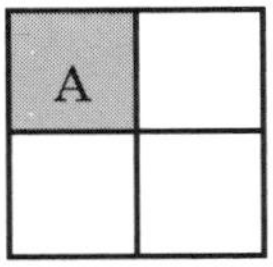

A

Here your main job is to make sure that the students know what they have to practise and to see that they practise it effectively. You will also want to check what they are doing.

Your role here, then, is that of CONDUCTOR (like the person in charge of the orchestra.)

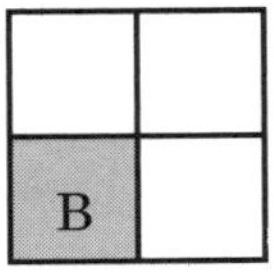

B

Here you have to organise the activities so that the students can practise in pairs. You also have carry out some checking while they are doing it.

Your role here, then, is that of ORGANISER and MONITOR.

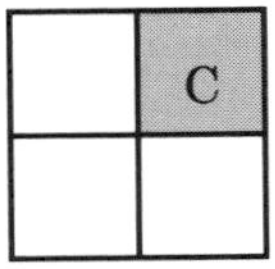

C

Remember that the main reason for taking part in fluency activities is to get the students to interact.

So we can say that your main role here is that of STIMULATOR.

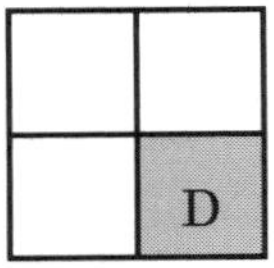

D

Here your main job is to set up the activities and to be available for help and advice *if* the students need and ask for it. You mustn't try to check these activities as in B.

Your role here, then, is that of MANAGER and CONSULTANT.

Keep these roles in mind as you teach. They will help to make all your classwork more effective.

Accuracy work with the whole class

Class arrangement

In a traditional classroom, the students sit in rows, as in Classroom A below. They face the teacher at the front of the classroom, so that when they do oral work, they have to speak to the backs of one another's heads! And when they do question and answer work, across the class, they look at the teacher while they are talking, not the student they are speaking to. Of course, they are also waiting for the teacher to tell them if they are right!

```
            T
XXX   XXX   XXX   XXX
XXX   XXX   XXX   XXX
XXX   XXX   XXX   XXX
XXX   XXX   XXX   XXX
```

Classroom A

If you can, then, try to arrange the students so that they face one another as far as possible, as in Classroom B below. This isn't ideal, because it is a large class, but at least most of the students can look at one another.

```
XX                 XX
XX        T        XX
XX                 XX
XXXXXXXXXXXXXXXXXXXXX
XXXXXXXXXXXXXXXXXXXXX
```

Classroom B

And if you really can't rearrange the classroom – because the desks are too heavy? Don't worry! You can still do good work with the whole class. Just remember to get your students to look at one another while they are asking and answering questions. Don't let them speak through *you*!

Ways of teaching the whole class

The main ways of doing this are:

- working with students individually (T:S or S:T);
- getting the students to work with one another (S:S);
- doing chorus work;
- doing team work.

Let's look at each of these in turn.

T:S

Here, then, you work with one student at a time, before or after chorus work, for example. You can do drills and language games in this way. But if you have a large class, it can be boring for most of the students, who know they will never get a chance to say anything.

What can we do about it? Here are some things to keep in mind:

- do it briskly and don't let it go on too long;
- let the students ask *you* questions too;
- choose students at random in the class, so that the students won't know whose turn it is going to be next.

S:S

But, under your direction, students can interact with one another across the class. This is often called 'open pairs'. It is a useful technique for dialogue repetition, question and answer work and many kinds of controlled drill. For example:

T: A, ask B what Ann was doing in the library.
A: What was Ann doing in the library?
B: She was looking for a book.

Or:

T: A . . . question with *where*.
B . . . answer.
A: Where did Ann go?
B: She went to the library.

But, once again, be brisk and don't do this kind of work for too long in a large class. Instead, move on to pair work.

Chorus work

You can use chorus work for dialogue repetition and for certain kinds of controlled drill (for example, the one on page 1). After you have presented a grammar point or some new vocabulary, you can give all the students a chance to say *something* through chorus work. (But don't assume that this is *all* that is needed to make sure they learn new material!)

Group the students in choruses according to where they are sitting in the classroom, as shown below. It doesn't matter if the chorus groups aren't all the same size. But make sure that the students know which group they belong to *before* you start to practise.

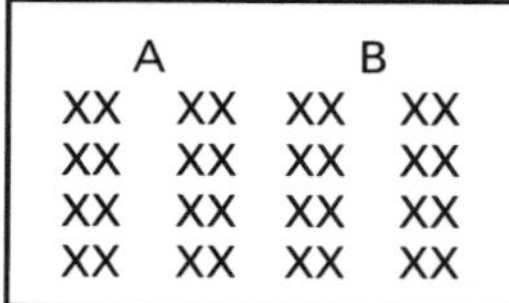

A B C
XXX XX XXX
XXX XX XXX
XXX XX XXX
XXX XX XXX

Some points to keep in mind

- speak clearly and repeat sentences, etc. if necessary;
- speak at normal speed;
- choose material for repetition carefully: sentences must be short enough for the students to say *together*;
- use gestures to tell the students when to start. Indicate stressed (i.e. important) syllables with a downward movement of the hand;
- control the noise level: signal to the class to make less noise or get them to stop and start again;
- listen out for mistakes;
- correct mistakes: stop the repetition and give the model again. If a sentence is difficult, get the students to repeat it bit by bit, starting at the end. For example: *in 'London, 'hat in 'London, ... I 'bought a 'new 'hat in 'London.*

Teams

As for chorus work, the students are divided into two or more groups – but the purpose is very different. As in a game of football, the teams will compete. For example, in a language game, like the one on page 1, a student from each team in turn tries to make a correct guess and so score a point for his team.

Team work can be a very effective way of involving the students in whole class activities, especially games. But make sure that the students do not get too competitive and so get out of control.

Whole class work: points to keep in mind

Remember that the students will be looking at *you* the whole time and also expecting guidance. Everything you do, therefore, during whole class practice will be important.

Stand at the front of the class. The students must be able to see and hear you (and also see any visual aid you are using). Don't move around more than necessary.

Look at the students. It is easier to control them if you have 'eye contact' with them.

Look interested in what they are saying. Don't forget to smile!

Watch the students while they are talking. Are they ... interested? ... bored? ... tired?

Control the class clearly and economically. Don't talk more than you have to. Use signals: for example, put your hand behind your ear to indicate *Listen*! Use simple instructions such as: *All together*! *Stop*!

Make sure the students get enough practice. If you have a large class, do a mixture of chorus and individual work. Then move on to pair work.

Examples of accuracy work with the whole class

Drills

We had an example of a drill on page 1. This is a very controlled or mechanical drill. The students don't have any choice in what they say. They don't have to *think* while they are speaking. So how do drills like this help the learners? By themselves, they certainly won't be enough to get them to learn grammar and vocabulary. But they do help with pronunciation. Learners need to be able to 'get their tongues round' structures and vocabulary. Drills can help to give them confidence – and this is important, at least from the students' point of view.

Doing drills in chorus

You can do mechanical drills in chorus, controlling them through keywords or pictures. In the drill below the teacher starts off by giving an example, which he gets Chorus A and Chorus B to repeat.

T: Listen!
Would you like to go to the cinema tonight?
No. We'd rather go to the disco.
Chorus A: question. Chorus B: answer. Ready?
(*T gestures to Chorus A to start.*)
CH A: Would you like to go to the cinema tonight?
CH B: No. We'd rather go to the disco.
T: Good. Now, A: SEASIDE – TOMORROW. B: PARK.
CH A: Would you like to go to the seaside tomorrow?
CH B: No. We'd rather go to the park. (etc.)

Even drills like the following, where the students have to modify a short conversation each time, can be done in chorus. Here the teacher has three chorus groups.

T: Listen!
Peter works a lot!
He works too much!
I wish he wouldn't work so much!
Now: ANN – EAT.
CH A: Ann eats a lot!
CH B: She eats too much!
CH C: I wish she wouldn't eat so much!
T: Now: DICK – TALK. (etc.)

Making drills more meaningful

You can make drills more meaningful by allowing the students some choice in what they say. But in that case, you can't do chorus work. You have to do these drills either T:S or S:S. For example, the following drill allows the students to answer *truthfully*. The teacher starts off by giving a model.

T: Listen!
I like playing tennis.
Answer: So do I! Or: I don't.
(*T gives other examples as necessary*.)
Ready? I like jogging.
(*T indicates students to respond*.)
A: So do I!
B: So do I!
C: I don't! (etc.)

You can also practise free responses in the whole class situation. For example, in the drill below, the teacher makes a suggestion and invites objections.

T: Let's go to the cinema.
A: It's too late.
B: There aren't any good films on.
C: We want to watch TV.

The teacher then goes on to make other suggestions: *Let's have a picnic tomorrow. / Why don't we go for a walk?* (etc.) (That's why it's a drill: the students can respond freely but they *have* to make objections.)

And of course you can also make drills more meaningful by using pictures to get responses from the students. In this way you don't put the words into the students' mouths. For example, with the picture cards below, you could practise:

T: Would you like (an orange)?
S: { Yes, thank you very much.
No, I'd rather have (a pear).

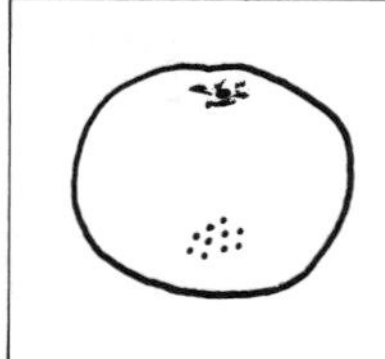

Points to watch

Drills needn't be totally controlled, then, and they certainly don't have to be boring. A lot will depend on how you do them with the class: make sure you do them in a lively way. All the same, don't forget that one reason for doing drills is to help the students use language more accurately. That means you must correct them if they make mistakes (e.g. by giving the correct model again or by getting another student to give the correct response and then asking the student who made a mistake to repeat the correct version.)

ACTIVITIES

1 Write more keywords for the two drills which you could do in chorus.

2 Write a 'meaningful' drill of your own.

Exercises

What do we mean by exercises? The term is used here for activities in the textbook which are based on a text the students have studied. They are often in the form of questions and answers, right-wrong statements and sentences for completion. They may even be in the form of a substitution table. For example:

Make true statements

John Kate Nick	can can't	swim sing play the guitar

Now, it's common practice to do exercises like this with the whole class. And also, unfortunately, waste quite a lot of class time too – if you *begin* with whole class work. It is much better to let the students prepare the answers first in pairs and then go over the exercise with the class. All the students are doing something at the pair work stage, and you can then go over the exercise more quickly and more efficiently.

> ACTIVITY
>
> Look at the exercises in your coursebook. Make a list of some that you could usefully get the students to do in pairs.

Language games

There are lots of traditional language games that you can do with the whole class and, as we have noted, they are a very good alternative to drills for many kinds of accuracy work. In fact they do the same thing as drills – they usually practise a bit of grammar or vocabulary or pronunciation – but in the form of a game. And because they are more enjoyable, the students remember things better. And they also lead on very naturally to pair work or informal group work.

We are going to look at two main types of games. But notice that you can adapt both of these to get a lot of different kinds of practice.

Sentence building

Probably the best known example of this is: *I went to the market and I bought* ... The students, playing individually or divided into teams, have to add a new word each time they say the sentence.

And of course they also have to remember all the words already used. For example:

T: I went to the market and I bought some apples.
A (*Team A*): I went to the market and I bought some apples and six oranges.
B (*Team B*): I went to the market and I bought some apples, six oranges and a kilo of potatoes. (etc.)

The game continues in this way until one of the players makes a mistake.

Even as it stands, the game can be used to practise different modifiers (*a*, *some*, *a kilo of*, *a box of*, etc.) and different vocabulary areas. But, very importantly, you can also change the sentence pattern. For example:

When I go to the market, I must buy .....
If you go to the market, will you buy .....?
When I went to the market, I should have bought .....

In addition to that, you can change the situation. For example:

When I go on holiday, I must remember to take with me .....
When the thieves broke into the office, they stole .....
If you had come earlier, you would have seen (Jack washing his hair) .....

If you want to control the game to some extent, put a list of possible items on the board for the students to choose from. You can get the students themselves to suggest the items.

socks	***sunglasses***	***hat***
jeans	***swimsuit***	***notebook***
toothbrush	***camera***	***sandals***

ACTIVITY

Suggest other ways of using this game, e.g. different sets of words and situations.

Guessing games

The game on page 1 is a guessing game: the students are trying to find out something they *don't know*. This is very different from a lot of question and answer work! The situations you use can be real or imaginary. It doesn't matter, for example, if your favourite colour, which the students are trying to find out, really is green or whether you are pretending.

There is really no limit to the number of guessing games you can make up in this way. The examples on pages 23–24 are just intended to give you some idea of the structures – elementary and advanced – and vocabulary that you can practise in this way. Try to think of other possibilities before you read on.

As you can see, guessing games of this kind don't need much preparation. Nor do they need any materials, unless you decide to use some pictorial material (see below).

You can also get the students to make their guesses in different ways. For example, they can use question tags (*You were born in February, weren't you?*) or statements (*I think / Perhaps you were born in October*).

If the students are trying to find out something about you, introduce extra bits of language in your responses, as in the example on page 1.

What am I going to do tonight?

You're probably going to watch TV!

Which month was I born in?

February, wasn't it?

It was June!

What would I like to be when I grow up?

An actor!

A teacher!

What would I have been doing if I hadn't come here?

I think you would have been playing tennis.

ACTIVITY

Make a list of structural and vocabulary items which you could practise through guessing activities. Think of the situations which you would use to present them as games to the students.

Guessing about pictures

You can also use visual material for guessing games of this kind. For example, you can ask the students to find out about a picture which they cannot see. Notice that the teacher first gives the class a 'clue'.

T: It's a picture of a man.
He's doing something.
A: Is he walking?
T: No. He isn't walking.
B: Is he running?
T: No.
C: Is he working, then?
T: Yes. He's working. But what kind of work is he doing?

In that game the students were using the same pattern each time: *Is he . . . ing?* You can also get the students to find out about a picture, using a variety of patterns. For example:

T: It's a picture of the seaside.
A: Are there many people there?
T: Yes. There are quite a lot.
B: Is the sun shining?
T: Yes, it is.
C: Is the seaside big? (etc.)

This is the kind of game you can get the students to play in teams. Give them a point for each correct guess.

ACTIVITY

Find or draw pictures suitable for this activity.

Listening

The following are examples of listening activities that you can do with the whole class. Notice that the students can interact with you while you are talking. The same picture is used for all three activities.

Picture description

Describe a picture but make deliberate mistakes while you are doing it. The students have to correct you. For example:

T: There are two trees in the picture.
A: No! There's only one.
T (*beginning again*): There's a tree in the picture. It's on the right. There's a woman under the tree.
B: That isn't right! It's a man.
T: There's a man under the tree. He's standing there.
C: No, he isn't. He's sitting there. (etc.)

ACTIVITY

Draw two or three pictures which you could use for this activity. Write out how you would describe the pictures to a class.

Picture dictation

Talk about a picture which the students cannot see and ask them to draw it while you talk. The students can ask questions about anything they don't understand. For example:

> There's a man under a tree. The man ... he ... is reading. He has his back against the tree. There are some birds in the picture, too. Three of them.

The sort of questions the students should ask are: *Where is the tree – on the left or on the right? Is the man sitting or standing? Is the man looking to the left or the right?* Without this information, they cannot draw the picture correctly.

Describe and note

This activity is similar to the one above, except that the students make notes while they are listening instead of trying to draw the picture. Again they should ask questions if something is not clear.

After they have made their notes, you can ask them to:
- compare their notes and draw the picture, working in pairs;
- give an oral description of the picture;
- write a description of the picture (working in pairs).

Word Bingo: a vocabulary revision activity

Vocabulary, especially sets such as the names of colours, months, food, occupations, hobbies, etc., needs frequent revision. The students learn easily – but they forget easily too! One way of revising vocabulary quickly and easily is through games – especially guessing games like those we have just looked at. But you can also do it through 'Word Bingo', which is a listening activity in the form of a game.

How to play Word Bingo Ask the students to give you the items in the set you want to revise. Write these on the board. Add some of your own if necessary. For example (for occupations):

postman	***secretary***	***artist***	***bus driver***
doctor	***lorry driver***	***teacher***	***taxi driver***
shopkeeper	***librarian***	***bank clerk***	***policeman***
dentist	***actor***	***footballer***	***fireman***

Twelve to sixteen items will usually be enough.

Ask the students to choose any six words and to write them down in a box, like this:

Student A	
actor	
dentist	
fireman	
footballer	
postman	
teacher	

Student B	
lorry driver	
postman	
librarian	
dentist	
artist	
actor	

Student A and Student B have chosen two words that are the same. Tell the students to listen carefully while you call out the words in the list *in any order*. The first student to hear all his six words read out shouts out 'Bingo!' and is the winner.

Repeat the activity once or twice, especially if the students are enjoying it.

> ACTIVITY
>
> Make a list of key vocabulary areas which you could practise through *Word Bingo*.

Writing

In real life, writing normally involves some interaction. We write letters and notes for people to read and reply to, for example. Unfortunately, in the classroom, most writing is done to be read – and *corrected*!

One simple way of getting the students to interact through writing is to ask them to write to one another in class. For example, they can ask for personal information. As for oral work, they will need a model (which can be written on the board).

Here are examples of the kind of things you can get students to write to one another.

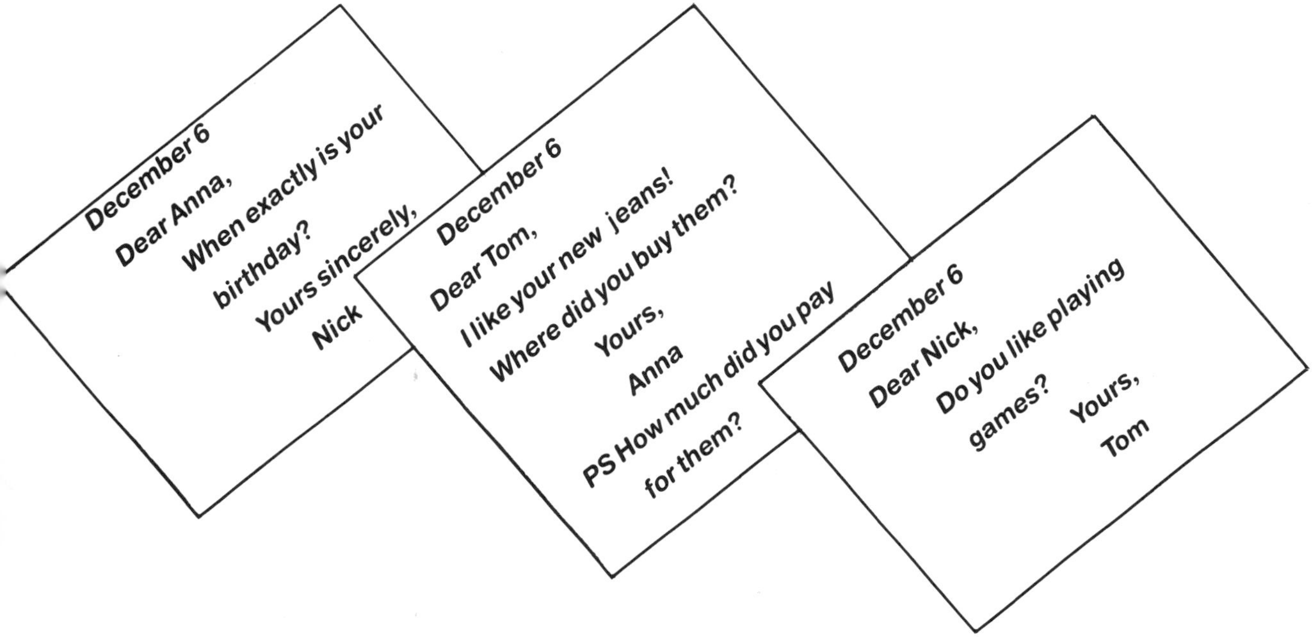

December 6
Dear Anna,
When exactly is your birthday?
Yours sincerely,
Nick

December 6
Dear Tom,
I like your new jeans!
Where did you buy them?
Yours,
Anna
PS How much did you pay for them?

December 6
Dear Nick,
Do you like playing games?
Yours,
Tom

Of course it is true that the students could more easily – and more naturally – find out this information orally, because the person they are writing to is present. But the important thing is that they *enjoy* this type of activity. It is partly the speed at which everything goes. They can write and answer several notes in just a few minutes. But another important factor is that they appreciate – perhaps for the first time – that they can actually communicate through writing (because they get an answer, not some corrections in red ink!). And of course they learn a good deal about letter writing in this way – where to put the address and the date, for example, and how to start and finish a letter.

One final point: it is important for *you* to join in the activity. It is one way of finding out if mistakes are being made. And the students enjoy finding out about you too – and perhaps will ask questions which they would not normally ask orally!

ACTIVITY

Make a list of other items which you could practise through this writing activity.

Controlled conversation

Finally, don't forget to *talk* to your students, as a class or individually, making as much use as you can of the language they know. You will sometimes get a chance to do this at the beginning of the lesson, while you are waiting for all the students to come. But you should also try to find time to chat to your students *during* the lesson – from time to time at least. Like this, for example:

T: I saw 'Clever Boy' on TV last night. Did anyone else see it?
A: Yes. I did.
B: Yes.
C: No. I went out.
T: Did you like it? A?
A: Not very much.
T: Really? Why not?
A: It was, er, too long. And I was tired!
T: Yes, it was quite long. But I liked it. How about you, B?
B: Yes, I liked it. It was funny. (etc.)

Conversations like this may not be very exciting. And they may sometimes seem like a distraction from the lesson, especially if you want to get on with something *really important*! But perhaps for the students they are more important than what is in the textbook. Because they show them that the language they are learning can be used to talk about something *personal*.

Accuracy work in pairs

Why pair work is necessary

Unless you have a very small class, you will never be able to give your students *enough* oral practice through whole class work. Suppose, for example, you have a class of thirty students (and that is not a *very* large class) and you do oral work for thirty minutes of the lesson. Then each student will be able to talk for *one* minute at the most – even if they do *all* the talking. On the other hand, if you divide your students into pairs for just five minutes, each student will get more talking time during those five minutes than during the rest of the lesson. From the learners' point of view, then, some pair work in the course of the lesson is absolutely essential.

Other advantages of pair work

- the learners get a chance to work independently: this is good for motivation and good preparation for group work, when they will have to take a lot of responsibility for what they do;
- they can face and talk directly to one another, so it is much closer to the way we use language outside the classroom;
- pair work provides some variety during the lesson. Two or three short pair work activities are a good way of breaking up the lesson.

What exactly is pair work?

Apart from 'open pairs', where the students talk to one another across the class under your control (see page 15), there are two main kinds of pair work.

Fixed pairs

This is when the students work with the same partner (usually the student on the left or the right) in order to complete a task of some

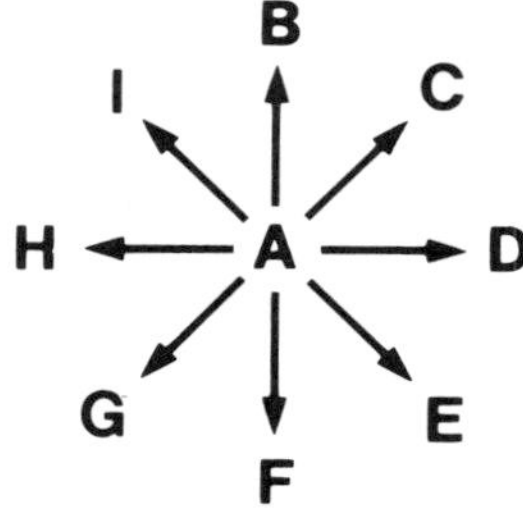

kind. This is how the students will practise the short dialogue on page 2, for example. Afterwards they may change partners, either to repeat the activity, or to do something connected with it. For example, for the questionnaire activity on page 2, the students first have to write the questionnaire (e.g. A works with B), then use it to interview someone (A works with C, B works with D) and finally report back to their original partners (A works with B again).

Most pair work activities you do will be of the 'fixed pairs' kind. And, if you want to keep things very simple at the start, choose activities where the students only interact with one partner.

Flexible pairs

For this the students keep changing partners. To give a simple example, each student may have to interview several others in order to find out two or three things about each (see the activity on page 2). For example: *Do you like animals? Have you got a pet? What (other) pets would you like to keep?* So A will interact as shown above.

If you are going to do flexible pair work, you must decide whether you can let the students stand up and move around the classroom freely. This will make the activity more interesting for them because *they* can then choose the person they want to talk to. But it may not be possible to do this in *your* classroom (or at least not very often), because it is too small or because the desks don't allow it. In that case the students will have to interact with those around them *without getting up*. This is not so exciting but at least it is a way of doing certain types of activity.

How to organise the class for pair work

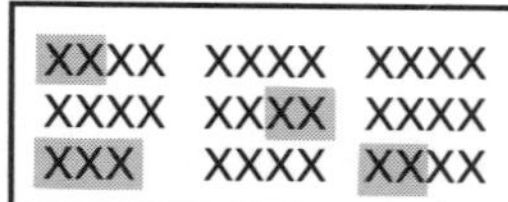

Classroom A

XXX XXX XXX
XXX XXX XXX
XXX XXX XXX

Classroom B

Very often you will want to move from class work to a related pair work activity – to give the students the extra practice they need at that stage. And you'll want the activity to follow on quickly, so you can't afford to spend a lot of valuable class time, moving students around so that they can work together. The time factor is especially important if you do pair work two or three times in a lesson.

As far as you can, then, use the existing classroom arrangement. Get the students to work with a neighbour and only move a student

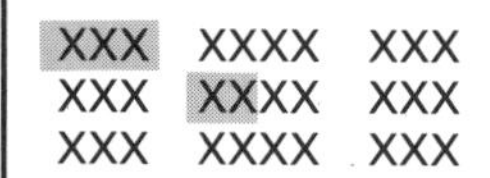

Classroom C

if it is absolutely necessary. This means that if the students are seated in twos or threes, as in Classrooms A and B, let them work in this way. Sometimes it may be a mixture of twos and threes as in Classroom C. The important thing is for the students to be able to form pairs quickly and without any fuss.

What happens if three students have to work together for pair work? For some activities, like practising a dialogue, they will have to take turns. A and B will practise first; then B and C and finally A and C. But this doesn't mean that one student is doing nothing while the other two are talking! On the contrary, the students have to get used to checking one another. So, while A and B are talking, C will control the activity and listen out for mistakes. Again, this is good preparation for group work, when the students will be completely on their own and will have to correct one another.

Problems with pair work

The students will make too much noise!

Let's look at some of the objections that are sometimes made to pair work.

Fifteen to twenty pairs of students practising at the same time *will* probably make quite a lot of noise! But unless the noise is likely to disturb the class next door, you could just ignore it. The noise certainly won't bother the students themselves. They will be too busy practising and in any case they can hear one another quite easily.

But, if you must control the noise level (because of the class in the next room), then stop the activity and ask the students to start again ... more quietly.

The students will make mistakes!

At this stage, since your aim is accuracy, you must try to prevent mistakes as much as possible. So give the students a clear model and give them enough practice *before* they start on their own. You should also write relevant material on the board. If, in spite of all this, you find that the students are making mistakes (or perhaps one serious mistake), then stop the pair work, repeat and practise the model again and then let the students carry on.

But can we be sure that some students aren't making mistakes? No, because you can't check everyone. But being able to give the students a lot of extra practice in this way is far more important than a few mistakes.

The students won't work properly!

Perhaps some students won't do the activity properly. They may simply chatter in their mother tongue – or do nothing at all! But you generally know which students in the class are most likely to do this, so you can take steps to deal with it. But it must be said that, just because some students *may* misbehave, this is not a good reason for not doing pair work. When you are teaching the whole class, you can't be sure that the students are co-operating just because they are keeping quiet.

My students expect me to teach them!

It is true that in some countries students (and parents) expect the teacher to stand in front of the class ... and 'teach'. That is, to control and instruct the students. In that case, they will probably expect other things too – lots of drills and no language games, for example.

Be prepared to justify procedures like pair work and group work and also certain activities such as games and songs. Sometimes this is just as important as explaining *how* to do something. If the students understand why they are doing something, they will probably do it better.

Pair work: points to keep in mind

Divide the students into pairs in the most convenient way possible.

Make sure the students know exactly what they have to do.

Give a clear model and adequate preparation. Explain in the mother tongue if necessary. Point out any special features of an activity: for example, the students may have to exchange roles during a dialogue.

Keep activities simple.

Remember: fifteen to twenty pairs of students have to be able to get it right – the first time!

Don't let activities go on too long.

For accuracy work, three to five minutes is a good length (though some activities, like writing questionnaires, may need more time). And don't let activities just drag on. Stop the activity when most students have had enough practice. You don't want students sitting around ... getting bored and restless.

Carry out selective checking.

This will tell you, in general, how well or badly the students are doing.

Control the noise level as necessary.

Provide feedback.

From your selective checking you may want to tell the students immediately how well or badly they have done. Alternatively, make a note of mistakes and reteach these items in a future lesson. Don't forget that the students may want to ask *you* questions – or tell you what *they* think of an activity.

Examples of accuracy work in pairs

Controlled conversation

We need to get the students used to *working in pairs* and to *talking to one another*. They also need plenty of practice in using typical features of spoken English such as:

- short form answers: *Yes, I can / No, he won't* (etc.)
- contracted forms: *doesn't / hasn't* (etc.)
- question tags: *That's mine, isn't it? / You went there, didn't you?*
- hesitation markers: *Well, ... / I mean, ... / Er ....* (etc.)

A simple and effective way of doing this is to give the students short model dialogues to practise, like the one on page 2. They can then modify these in various ways when they practise in pairs.

Generally the dialogues should be about four to six lines long. They must include grammatical items and vocabulary which the students need to master as well as the colloquial items mentioned above.

Remember to make sure that the students can say the model dialogue confidently and accurately before they start to practise. So write it on the board and get them to say it after you, first of all in chorus and then in 'open pairs' across the class. Try out some of the variations as necessary.

Here are some ways of getting the students to modify the model dialogue.

a) **Give keywords for alternatives.**

A: Are you doing anything *tonight*?
B: I don't think so. Why?
A: Well, let's *go swimming*, then.
B: Mm. OK, if you like.

tonight	*go swimming*
this afternoon	have a game of tennis
tomorrow	play pingpong
on Sunday afternoon	go for a walk

b) **Draw a picture on the board.**

Make it simple, like the one below. This shows people doing things at the seaside.

You can use a picture like this to get the students to practise very different dialogues, like the two below. Notice that the second one is very colloquial.

A: I was looking for you *this morning*.
B: Were you? Well, I went to the beach.
A: What were you doing there?
B: Oh, I *was swimming*.

A: Seen Jack?
B: He's gone to the beach, I imagine.
A: I wonder what he's doing . . .
B: Can't you guess? He's probably *playing football* – as usual!

c) **Draw a map on the board.**

The one below is a town plan.

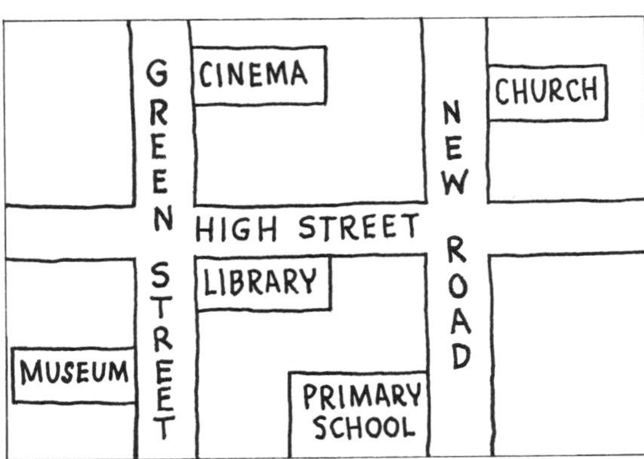

The students can use the map like the picture in b). For example:

A: Is there a museum in Newtown?
B: Yes, of course. It's in *New Road*.
A: *New Road*? Are you sure?
B: Oh, sorry! It's in *Green Street*.

d) **Give the students information in tables.**

JOHN BELL	32	SHOP ASSISTANT	FOOTBALL, PHOTOGRAPHY
MARY HILL	27	HAIRDRESSER	TRAVEL, READING

One simple practice model could be:

A: How old is *John Bell*?
B: John Bell? Let me see ... He's *thirty-two*.
A: And what does he do?
B: He's a *shop assistant*.
A: And what does he do in his spare time?
B: Oh, he's interested in *football* and *photography*.

e) **Get the students to talk about themselves.**

This is important for two reasons:
- they will often prefer to do this;
- they don't need any variations. They can produce them from their own experience or make them up quite easily.

Here are some examples.

A: Where were you at *six o'clock on Sunday*?
B: Let me think ... Ah, yes! I was *at home*.
A: Do you remember what you were doing?
B: Of course. I was *watching TV*.

A: Have you ever been abroad?
B: Yes. I went *last year*.
A: Where to?
B: *France*.

For this the students may need an alternative, in case they haven't been abroad.

A: Have you ever been abroad?
B: No, never.
A: Would you like to?
B: Yes, of course!
A: Where would you like to go?
B: To *India*!

ACTIVITIES

1 Write other model dialogues for the picture on page 37 and the map on page 37.

2 Continue the table on page 38 and suggest other uses for it.

3 Write other model dialogues like the ones on page 38 which the students could use for talking about themselves.

Role play activities

Role play involves *pretending*: we ask the students to imagine that they are *someone* else (a tourist, a customer in a shop) or *somewhere* else (in the street, at the doctor's). Role play is a way of taking the students out of the classroom for a while and showing them how English can be useful to them in certain situations. But we have to be careful. Not all students find it easy to pretend to be someone else. Also we don't want them to make a lot of mistakes at the accuracy stage. So remember to:

- keep the situation simple;
- provide essential language.

In fact some of the dialogue activities we have just looked at involve a small amount of role play. And you could use some of the materials in b) to d) to introduce more. For example, the street plan in c) can be used for a role play situation involving asking for and giving directions.

IMAGINE THAT YOU HAVE JUST ARRIVED IN NEWTOWN. YOU ARE AT THE MUSEUM AND YOU WANT TO KNOW HOW TO GET TO THE CHURCH. STOP A PASSER-BY AND ASK.

For this activity you will probably need to give the students a model dialogue and you must certainly make sure that they have all the necessary alternative expressions: *Go straight ahead / Turn (left) / It's on the (left) hand side of the road.*

Here are some ways of guiding role play situations.

a) **Use visual material.**

Menus like this, can easily be copied from the board. Ask the students to imagine that they are in a cafe. They can then:

Tea	***25p***
Coffee	***35p***
Milk	***20p***
Sandwich	***40p***
Cake	***25p***
Biscuits	***10p each***

- discuss what they are going to have to eat and drink:

A: What are you you going to have, then?
B: Me? Oh, I think I'll have a cup of tea and a sandwich. How about you?
A: Oh, I'll have a cup of tea too and a cake.

- persuade someone to have something:

A: What would you like, then?
B: Oh, just a cup of coffee.
A: Is that all? Why don't you have something to eat?
B: But I'm not hungry!
A: Oh, come on! Have a cake! They're very good! (etc.)

Programmes (*radio, TV, events*) are also very useful. Write simple ones on the board, with the help of suggestions from the students.

The students can:

- talk about programmes which they have watched:

CHANNEL 1	
6	SCIENCE REPORT
6.30	TODAY'S SPORT
7	TOP OF THE POPS
8	FILM: THE LAST MAN ON EARTH
9	NEWS

CHANNEL 2	
6	NEWS
6.30	LOOKING AT BOOKS
7	MOTOR RACING
8.15	PLAY: HAPPY DAYS
9	HISTORY: EVERYDAY LIFE IN SHAKESPEARE'S DAY

A: Did you see *'The Last Man on Earth' on Channel 1* last night?
B: No. I *went out*. What was it like it?
A: It was *very good*.

A: Did you watch the *history programme on Channel 2* last night?
B: No. What time was it on?
A: It started at *nine*.
B: Oh, I was watching *the news* at that time.

- talk about programmes they are going to watch:

A: What shall we watch on TV tonight?
B: Well, I'd like to watch *'Top of the Pops'*.
A: What time is it on?
B: From *seven to eight on Channel 1*.
A: Oh! I'd like to see *the motor racing on Channel 2*.
B: All right, then. Let's watch that instead. Now, what shall we watch after that? (etc.)

Agendas (or diaries) are another useful practice device. Ask the students to copy the blank agenda from the board and to fill in four days on which they are going to be busy. If necessary, give some suggestions (like those in the completed agendas below).

Student A

MON	***work in library***
TUES	
WED	***go shopping***
THURS	***meet P. at airport***
FRI	
SAT	***visit Uncle T.***
SUN	

Student B

MON	
TUES	***go to Bristol***
WED	
THURS	***visit J in hospital***
FRI	
SAT	***go shopping***
SUN	***PICNIC!***

The students then talk to one another to find out a day on which they are both free. For example:

A: Why don't we play tennis one day next week?
B: That's a good idea. Well, *I'm* free on Monday.
A: Oh, I'm not. I've got to work in the library on Monday. How about Tuesday?
B: Tuesday? Sorry! I'm going to visit some friends in Bristol on Tuesday. (etc.)

b) **Give the students a situation like the one below.**

YOU HAVE LOST YOUR BAG. GO TO THE LOST PROPERTY OFFICE TO SEE IF ANYONE HAS HANDED IT IN. ANSWER THE QUESTIONS THE MAN THERE ASKS YOU.

The questions below are in the form of an incomplete dialogue. The students first work out the details of the object they have lost. They then take it in turns to go to the Lost Property Office and ask for it. B is the man who works in the Lost Property Office.

A: Er, I've lost my bag.
B: A bag? We've got dozens of bags! What kind of bag?
A: .....
B: What colour is it?
A: .....
B: Is it old or new?
A: .....
B: And what size is it?
A: .....
B: What was in it?
A: .....
B: Oh, and by the way, where did you lose it?
A: .....

ACTIVITIES

1 Write a model dialogue for the role play activity on page 40 (asking for and giving directions).

2 Write other model dialogues for the menu on page 40 and the TV programme on page 41.

3 Write agendas like the one on page 41 for:
a) two tourists who want to spend an afternoon together;
b) two businessmen who want to arrange a weekday meeting.

4 Write an incomplete dialogue like the one on page 42 for an umbrella.

Games

We have already seen how effective games – especially guessing games – can be for class practice. They can be equally effective for pair work, too, and when you have done a guessing game with the class, you can usually ask the students to go on practising it in pairs. In this way you can be reasonably sure that they won't make a lot of mistakes.

However, for guessing activities in pairs, you will be able to give the students a lot more practice if you use some visual material. Here are some suggestions. Notice that you can generally use this material for other activities too. The small object sheet on this page can be used again and again.

a) **Use small object picture sheets.**

You will need to make a class set (about fifteen to twenty copies) unless you can get the students to draw their own.

A can ask B to guess which object(s):

- he is thinking of (*Is it the* .....?)

- he is going to give him for his birthday (*Are you going to give me a .....?*)
- he would like for his birthday (*Would you like a .....?*)
- he has got at home (*Have you got a .....?*)

The students can also work in pairs to:

- *find different uses for the objects*. For example:
  tennis racquet: play tennis / catch fish / collect flowers
- *link different objects*. For example:
  bike – cake: I'm going to use the bike to go to the baker's to buy a cake.
- *link objects with people*. (e.g. scissors – hairdresser) *or with places* (book – library)
- *put the objects in order*. For example: alphabetical, biggest / smallest, heaviest / lightest (etc.)
- *put the objects into categories*. For example: things that you normally find in the (kitchen), use (every day), take on holiday (etc.)

For activities like these, where the students have to make decisions, get them to compare their ideas with another pair.

You can also do some class work as follow-up.

In addition, you can use the picture sheet to play the sentence building game on page 22. Tell the students to cover up each object after they have used it in their sentence.

Finally, you can use the picture sheet for playing board games. That is why the squares are numbered 1–16. The players start on S (= Start) next to square 1 and move round the board to H (= Home). They throw a dice in order to move and when they land on a square, they must carry out a task (see below). If they cannot do the task, they must stay where they are.

For each game choose one of the following tasks:

- name the object
- spell the name of the object
- say something about the object
- give one or more uses for the object
- say what you would do with the object if you had it
- make up a sentence using the object
- link the object with the one on the square you have just left

ACTIVITIES

1 Make a list of items for another small object picture sheet like the one on page 43.

2 Using a dice, play the various versions of the board game suggested on page 44. Decide at what level you could use these versions.

b) Use small picture cards.

These are similar to the ones that can be used for the whole class activity on page 20. Make a class set of these with small pictures cut out of magazines or travel brochures. Stick each picture on a piece of card (about the size of a postcard).

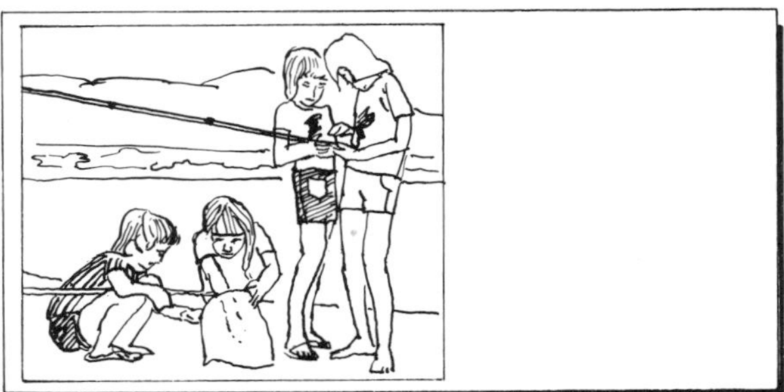

The students can use these cards to:

- try to find out about each other's pictures by asking questions. For example: *Are there any people in your picture? Are they men? Are they working?* (etc.)
- play a memory game. For example: they look at a card for a minute, turn it face downwards on the desk and try to remember as many details as possible in the picture.
- compare two cards to say what the differences and similarities are. For example: *There's a . . . in this picture, but not in this one / There's a . . . in both these pictures / There's a . . . in both these pictures, but the one in this picture is (bigger, green, etc.).*

c) Get the students to make their own pictures.

Give them some sort of outline for their pictures, like the ones below, together with a list of objects to draw in their pictures.

Tell them they can omit two or three objects on the list. This means that each student will draw slightly different pictures – because they will put the objects in different positions and they will use different objects.

B's picture

A's picture

With the help of pictures like these (quickly drawn) the students can work in pairs to:

- find out about each other's pictures by asking questions. For example:

  A: Where have you put your trees?
  B: I've put them between the two houses. How about you?
  A: I've only put one tree in my picture.
  B: Where is it? (etc.)

- compare the pictures they have drawn. That is, instead of trying to find out about each other's pictures, they place them side by side and talk about the differences. For example:

  A: Oh, you've put all your birds on the trees.
  B: That's right. Where are yours?
  A: They're here, in the sky, flying over the house. The small one. And here's my cloud – in the corner. I've only drawn one.
  A: I've drawn two. They're both over the big house.
  B: And they're big ones too! (etc.)

> ACTIVITY
>
> Draw other 'outline' pictures like the ones on page 46. For example, for a street, a beach and a park. Make a list of the objects which the students must draw in their pictures.

Questionnaires and quizzes

Questionnaires like the ones below are an effective way of getting the students to ask *real* questions.

S asks: *Can you .....?*

	BILL	JEAN
swim	YES	YES
play tennis	NO	
play chess	NO	

S asks: *Have you seen .....?*
Did you like it?

	Name: Maria	
	Q1	Q2
JAWS 2	Yes	No
GHOSTBUSTERS	Yes	Yes
RAMBO	No	

You may have to prepare the class for this activity. For the first questionnaire, for example, get some suggestions from the class, write them on the board (perhaps asking the students how to spell them too) and tell them that they can add ideas of their own when they write their questionnaires. It may also be necessary to check that the students can ask the interview questions correctly. For example, you could use the first questionnaire to get the students to practise asking: *How often do you . . . ?* with the answers: *sometimes, occasionally, hardly ever*, etc. Perhaps a new use of frequency adverbs for them! This will require quite careful class preparation.

Don't forget that the students should report back to their partners afterwards (see page 2 for the stages of this activity). This means that they will be telling one another things like: *Bill can swim, but he cannot play the piano, and he cannot play chess.* You may also like to carry out a class survey afterwards, to find out how many students can do something.

There is another type of questionnaire that involves flexible pair work (see page 32). For the questionnaire below, for example, the student has to ask as many others as possible.

S has to find out who: . . . . .

	1 ANN	2 TOM	3
CAN COOK	Yes	Yes	
HAS A DOG	No	Yes	
GETS UP EARLY	No	Yes	
LIKES SCHOOL	Yes	No	

However, he can do this by asking the students who are sitting nearest to him.

Questionnaires can involve finding out detailed information, like the one above and the one below, where the 'interviewer' is trying to find out about eating habits. He first completes the section about himself.

S asks: *What do you have for . . . . . ?*
or: *What did you have for . . . . . (yesterday)?*

	BREAKFAST	LUNCH	DINNER
SELF			
JEAN			
BILL			

Quizzes are similar to questionnaires, but the answers are generally factual. The quiz below, for example, is on 'general knowledge'.

1 What is the capital of Spain?	
2 What languages do they speak in Switzerland?	
3 Where is the Sahara desert?	
4 Who invented the telephone?	
5 When was Gandhi born?	

Quizzes like this involve almost as much writing as talking, but if you ask the students to work in pairs, they *have* to talk in order to write their quiz. Then, if the pairs exchange quizzes, they *have* to talk in order to agree about the answers. But that's not all. Look at the stages below:

1 A and B write their quiz.
2 They exchange their quiz with C and D. They talk about and write down the answers to C and D's quiz.
3 A and B get their own quiz back from C and D and check what C and D have written. They tell C and D their results.

You can also get the students to write quizzes about one another (for example: *What's Tim's telephone number? Was Ann born in this town?* etc.), which could involve some moving around in the classroom to get the answers.

ACTIVITIES

1 Add more items to each of the questionnaires in this section.
2 Write other questionnaires and quizzes of your own.

'Find a partner' activities

These involve 'flexible' pair work because each student has to find a 'mate' of some kind – someone who has made the same decision. For example, the task might be:

Decide when you are going to the park and what you are going to do there.

The students have to choose from the following possibilities, which you write on the board:

TIME	ACTIVITIES
morning	sit and read
afternoon	jog
evening	climb trees
	play tennis

Since there are only twelve possibilities, each student is likely to find a partner. However, if you don't want the students to get up and move around the classroom, reduce the possibilities to nine by taking out one of the activities.

In order to find a partner, each student has to ask a number of students in turn: *When are you going to the park?* (or: *Are you going to the park in the (morning)?*) and: *What are you going to do there?* (or: *Are you going to (climb trees)?*). He does this until he finds someone who has made the same decision. He can then say: *'Let's go together, then!'*

Similarly, the students may be asked to find someone who has the same likes and dislikes. For the activity below, first ask the students to suggest the items and write them on the board. Each student must first write down his own likes and dislikes before he starts interviewing.

S asks: *Do you like .....?*

	SELF	1 Nick	2 Maria	3 Ann
cats	×			
TV	√			
reading	√			
coffee	√			
cars	×			
rain	×			

Other skills

Listening

Students cannot actually listen in pairs, of course, but they can collaborate on a task which follows on from listening. For example, they can agree an answer or compare their answers. They can also use their notes to write something. Even if the coursebook does not suggest this, you should try it if you think it will make the activity more interesting for the students, or produce more interesting results.

However, from the point of view of developing listening, one important aspect of pair work is that it gets students used to *listening to one another* – not just to the teacher! Once again, it is good preparation for group work, when the students really will have to listen to one another.

Reading

When the students have read a text (silently, of course), they can be asked to do the related tasks together, unless you particularly want to test individual comprehension.

The students can also be asked to work in pairs to correct one another's exercises or homework from time to time. This is also a good reading comprehension activity.

Writing

Students often enjoy writing activities more if you let them collaborate. This is partly because they feel less isolated and because they get ideas from one another.

Here are some of the things you can ask students to do together:

- *write notes and letters to one another in class* (see page 29). For example, an invitation to a joint party. Both students sign the letter, but it is only addressed to one person.
- *write questionnaires and quizzes.*
- *write questions (or other exercises) on a text.* This can be a pleasant change from using those in the coursebook!

- *do other types of writing activity which focus on accuracy* such as:
  - ▷ completing or writing texts (including dialogues like the one on page 42);
  - ▷ making sentences from jumbled words and making paragraphs from jumbled sentences (the students can also write these exercises for one another);
  - ▷ writing parallel texts. That is, the students have a model paragraph and have to write similar paragraphs with the help of keywords.

Fluency work with the whole class

In this chapter – and for the rest of the book – we are going to look at activities of a very different kind: the ones we use when we want the learners to use language *freely* – to express their *own* ideas and to say what *they* want. These activities show the learners that language is useful to them – not just another subject on the timetable – because they can *do something with it*. They also prepare them for using language in the real world *outside* the classroom.

Both these factors will motivate the learners – and make them want to go on learning.

Why do fluency work with the whole class?

But to get the students to use language freely and to try to express their own ideas, don't we need to leave them on their own, to work in pairs or groups? Surely they will get *more* opportunities to talk in this way and, very importantly, they won't feel that the teacher is listening in to them, waiting to correct any mistakes. So why do fluency work with the whole class? Isn't it a contradiction?

Of course *most* fluency work will be done in groups (see Chapters 9 and 10), but there are some things you can and should do with the whole class together. Why is this? Simply, because *you* have something to contribute. For accuracy work, you helped the students by giving them good models, by explaining things and by correcting them when necessary. You did what teachers generally do in the classroom. Now you must help them by *showing* them that they can do things with the language – especially *talk*. Instead of being a teacher, you'll now have to be an ordinary human being!

Talk to your students!

You have probably been told: use recorded material as much as you can. It helps to bring the language – and the lesson – alive and it gives the students a chance to listen to many varieties of the language, not just *you*. And of course you can play the material over and over again. All this is very true: the cassette recorder can do many things that *you* can't do.

But there is something that *you* can do that the cassette recorder can't: you can *interact* with the students. The students can listen to the cassette recorder; they can even answer questions which it puts to them – but they cannot actually talk to it. They cannot exchange ideas with it.

This is where *you* come in. You can *talk* to the students. You can *listen* and *respond* to their ideas. You can *tell* them *jokes and stories*, and get them to do the same. You can *explain things* to the students. In short, you can do in the classroom most of the things that people normally do with language in the real world. And don't forget: you may be the *only* person who can do this with the students. You may be their *only* contact with the living language.

How you can help the students

That is why on these occasions you mustn't behave like a teacher – otherwise the students won't want to talk to you or to talk to one another while you are there. But at the same time, because you *are* their teacher, you will know how to help them. For example, you know what their language level is. So, when you are talking to them, you can adjust what you are saying to suit them, sometimes saying things in more than one way if necessary. And you can also deliberately make things a little more difficult, so that the students have to listen more carefully and try to guess the meaning. But, because you are able to watch their faces, you know exactly how far you can go. The cassette recorder can't do any of these things!

Get the students to interact.

And this is not the only way you can help the students – by talking to them, telling them stories and so on. You will often want *them* to do most of the talking, as, for example, in the discussion on page 3.

Your job then is to help the students to interact. You will join in just enough to keep the discussion going, by asking a question or contributing an idea, so as to encourage the students to join in. All this will require quite a lot of skill.

Get everyone to join in.

During whole class fluency work the students won't be doing so much talking as they could in groups. Much of the time, because of the size of the class, they will be *listening*, either to you or to one another. All the same, it is important that they should join in as much as possible. So you will need to make sure that the most talkative students don't dominate the activities. This is one of the problems with whole class discussion: a few students – the most talkative ones, the least shy ones – tend to do all the talking. You must encourage everyone to join in.

Listen to their ideas ...

Generally, then, during whole class fluency work, you won't have an easy time. This is mainly because you must try to behave more like a friend than a teacher. You must make the students feel that their ideas are just as interesting and just as important as yours. They must feel that you, like the other students in the class, are listening to *what* they say rather than *how* they say it.

... but listen to their language too.

But of course you can't help listening to their language and, once you get the students to talk freely, this is an excellent opportunity to find out how good they really are. When they are doing group work, it isn't always easy to hear if the students are making mistakes or what kind of mistakes they are making. But you can do this during fluency work with the class. As a rule, though, don't correct the students, unless you can do this indirectly (for example, by saying the same thing in a different way). Instead, make a note of any serious mistakes and reteach these points in a future lesson.

How often and how long?

A lot will depend on the level of the class and on the activity itself. Discussion, for example, will normally be a group activity, but *some* class discussion is an important follow-up for many group activities (see Chapter 9). Story-telling, on the other hand, *needs* a whole class audience and could go on as long as the students enjoy it. Similarly, some games are best played with the whole class.

In general, however, you probably won't want to do class fluency work as often as accuracy work with the class or pair work – although this doesn't mean that it is less important. It has its own part to play in helping students to learn a language. And to some extent, you may not always be able to plan it. The opportunity for talk or to tell a story or to have a discussion simply *happens*. And, if this is the case, you should welcome it – and let it go on for as long as the students are interested.

Examples of fluency work with the whole class

Conversation

Of course you can't have a *real* conversation with a class of sixty, fifty . . . or even twenty students. But, as we noted at the end of Chapter 4, you do need to talk to your students in a personal way from time to time. You need to ask them about what they have been doing (and to get them to ask you too), or to find out their opinions about something topical – the weather, a popular TV programme, a strike and so on.

You can do this by *deliberately* making use of certain bits of language – perhaps a new tense or some vocabulary the students learnt in a recent lesson. This is *accuracy* practice. Or you can talk to them in a relaxed way, as you would in a conversation *outside* the classroom, encouraging them to join in without worrying about mistakes. This is what is needed for *fluency* work. And you should be able to do it more frequently as the students make progress.

How does it help the students?

Obviously they cannot all join in. The main advantage for them is that they *hear* a live speaker who is interacting with them. This is something they can't get from recorded materials. They don't know the people who are talking and they can't join in. Also, when you talk to them in this way, they can get a better idea of what *they* can do with the language. And, because you are exchanging ideas, it helps to create a better relationship between you and the students.

When?

As with controlled conversation (page 30), there is usually something you can talk about at the beginning of the lesson. For example:

T: That's a nice sweater you're wearing, A.
A: Oh? Do you like it?
T: Yes, really. Where did you get it, by the way? (etc.)

This might lead on to talking about a new clothes shop that has opened – which will probably bring in other students.

Sometimes you can get a little conversation going by saying things like: *I went to a fantastic party last night*; or: *I don't feel very well this morning!* It doesn't matter if these remarks are true or not provided they catch the interest of the students and get them talking.

There is often a minute or two at the end of the lesson which you can fill in with something personal (for example, by asking the students if they are going to see a certain film or what they are planning to do at the weekend, etc.).

And sometimes a conversation may start up during the lesson, because of something you have come across in the textbook or a reader.

> Do we see the future in our dreams? Dr Ernest Young believes that we do. "Our dreams mix together events from the past, the present and the near future," he writes. "So, in a dream, we may see something before it has actually happened in real life."

If students are *really* reading with interest, you must expect a reaction to an idea like this – not just whether they agree or not but also whether they have had or heard about any strange dreams. This, then, should lead on to some conversation.

> ACTIVITY
>
> Make a list of ways of starting an informal conversation with the class. In particular, think of things you could chat to the students about at the beginning of the lesson.

Discussion

What is discussion?

Simply, any exchange of opinions or ideas. It is not always possible (or necessary) to distinguish it from conversation, which we have just been talking about.

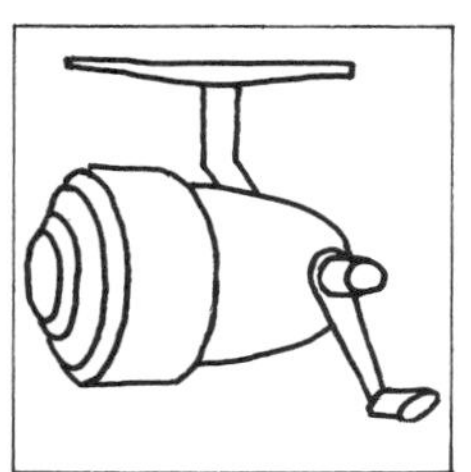

We have an example of a discussion on page 3. That was about a *topic*: whether young people spend too much money on clothes. But a discussion, in classroom terms, can be much simpler than that. You might show the class a picture of a strange looking object – and ask them what they think it is used for. This should be enough to elicit a string of suggestions – and objections. And that would be a discussion – whether it goes on for two minutes or twenty-two minutes.

Some problems

One is the same as we had with conversation: not *all* the students will be able to join in. That's why you should normally do discussion in groups – so that everyone gets a chance and wants to join in. Class discussion is a very useful and important follow-up to this (see page 81).

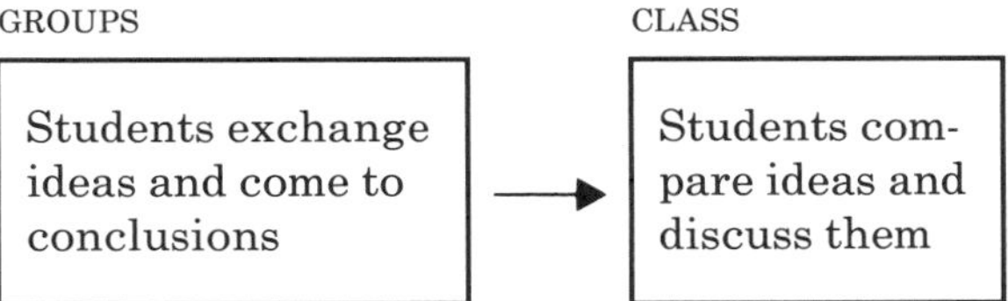

All the same, it helps to have some class discussion for its own sake from time to time. It gives you a chance to join in and to help the students to interact. And you can of course find out a great deal about them during a discussion – both their ideas and their control of the language.

How to start a discussion

Sometimes discussions – like conversations – will just 'happen', and this is a good thing (even if you are a little worried because your lesson is not going according to plan) because both you and the students will talk naturally. But you will also want to provoke a discussion from time to time. How do you do that?

Topics

Giving the class a 'topic' to talk about is the traditional way of starting a discussion. But if we begin to discuss a topic (education, advertising, politics, ...) in real life, it is usually because *something* has provoked us. For example, perhaps we have just seen an advertisement or read an article which annoys us. So in the classroom, too, if we want the students to talk about a topic, we must find some way of involving them in it. Some possibilities are:

Questions What's the real purpose of education?
Does everyone need the same education?

Provocative statements You can quote an opinion you have heard. For example:

> The other day, I heard someone say that for most people education is just a waste of time!

A text to read (e.g. a cutting from a newspaper) or a recording would be even better for this purpose.

Visual material This can be in the form of relevant pictorial material (posters, photographs, advertisements, etc.), which will help bring some aspect of the topic alive. Or you can use charts and diagrams to focus on some particular aspect of a topic. For example, you could compare the amount of money spent on education and defence.

ACTIVITY

Here are some possible topics:

keeping fit
saving money
choosing a career
helping old people
passing exams
becoming famous
making money

Choose one of these and decide how you would get students involved in it.

Other ways of starting a discussion

However, discussion needn't be about topics, especially if you only want a few minutes' talk. Here are some ways of getting the students to give their ideas and start arguing. We will look at most of these in more detail in Chapter 10.

- *play a song or read a poem.* Ask: *Is it good or bad? Does it have a 'message'? What?*
- *show a picture.* Ask: *What do you think it is about?*
- *show an object.* Ask: *What is it? What is it used for? What other things could it be used for? Who (do you think) made it?*
- *play a short sequence of sounds.* For example: footsteps, a splash, footsteps. Ask: *What do you think happened?*
- *play a very short conversation.* Ask: *Who is speaking? About what?*
- *present a problem.* For example: *How could you live for a week on (£20)? What other uses could you find for this classroom? Plan a picnic for (25) people.*

Sharing knowledge

Although this is not strictly discussion, asking the students to share their knowledge is a very good way of getting them to talk in a class situation – and will usually result in some argument over facts.

For example, you can get the class to tell you all they know about:

- *people:* Napoleon, Princess Diana, Einstein
- *places:* Australia, the Himalayas, Vesuvius
- *events:* the Olympic Games, the Second World War

ACTIVITY

Think of more areas (like people, places and events) where you can get the students to share their knowledge. Try to think of national and local ones too.

Simulation

What is a simulation? Let's imagine that you have given the students a problem to discuss. For example:

> A piece of land in the centre of the city has become available for a park. Decide what facilities you would like your park to have.

A piece of visual material, like the map below, will help to bring the problem alive. Although this is an imaginary situation, if you ask the students simply to work out a list of facilities, you will have only a *discussion* – and perhaps for some classes this would be quite enough.

Suppose, however, we introduce some role play, by giving the students parts to play like those below. And we also tell the students: there is going to be a public meeting at the Town Hall on Saturday, March 17th.

J. BLACK You are a keen football fan. You want to spend a lot of money on a good football pitch for teenagers. You don't want facilities for young children – or flower beds! You are an important man in the town. Express your opinions strongly!

H. WHITE You are a parent with six young children. You live in the area (J Black doesn't, by the way) and you know that there are a lot of people who would like a park for young children. There have been some bad accidents recently.

P. HEAD You are an old age pensioner. You would like a park where people of all ages can go and enjoy some peace. Stand up and express your opinions towards the end of the meeting.

We have now transformed the discussion into a *simulation*. The students are no longer free to be themselves. They have to play certain parts according to the instructions they have been given. Perhaps we won't get *more* talk, but we will get a very different kind of discussion from the one where the students are merely working out a list of facilities.

How do we involve all the students in the class?

We cannot give everybody in the class a speaking role, like those on the cards above, even if it is quite a small class of twenty to twenty-five students. The simulation will become too long and too complicated. Perhaps only about ten students will get speaking roles. So isn't simulation better as a group activity?

Simulations can be done in groups but, because it is more complicated than discussion, you will normally have to supervise it – if only to make sure that things don't go wrong. Besides, it is also the kind of activity where you would probably like to know how well the students are doing. The solution seems to be to do simulations as a class activity – but to try to involve everybody in some way.

For example, we can divide the class up like this:

MAIN SPEAKERS	MINOR SPEAKERS
REPORTERS	AUDIENCE

Let's see what each of these groups has to do:

Main speakers These are the ones, like J. Black, who will do most of the speaking, because they have some special interest in the park. Other speakers, for example, could include the mayor (who may be for or against the park), the finance officer (who perhaps doesn't want to spend a lot of money), a member of the city traffic committee (who would like a *car* park!), a member of the children's welfare committee (who would like the park to provide facilities especially for young children) and so on. These are the speakers who will provide most of the interaction.

Minor speakers These are the ones, like P. Head, who will join in from time to time – by asking questions or by interrupting the speakers.

Reporters These are the ones who have come to the meeting in order to write about it afterwards – for example, for newspapers, radio – and perhaps the school magazine. They won't take part in the discussion, but they will have to listen and take notes.

Audience These are the ones who won't take any active part in the meeting. Like members of the general public, they will sit and listen. Of course we can get them to react by cheering, etc.

The simulation itself, then, will be like a kind of debate. Your role is to see that it keeps going. You could even act as chairman of the meeting in order to see that both main and minor speakers join in.

The simulation could lead on to related writing tasks. For example, the main speakers can write reports and the reporters can write articles. Minor speakers and members of the audience can share these tasks with them.

Are simulations worthwhile?

Clearly they require more preparation and organisation than straightforward discussion. You have to prepare role cards. assign roles, guide the students in preparing for their roles and see that they keep to their roles during the simulation. Simulations also need more time. Perhaps a couple of lessons: one for preparation and one for the simulation itself. Discussing facilities for the park, on the other hand (as a class or group activity) could be done in ten or fifteen minutes. But they can be fun and, if you would like to give the students a challenge and a change, why not do a simulation once or twice a year?

ACTIVITY

Write more role cards like those on page 62. Make sure that they provide different opinions. You can use some of the suggestions for main speakers on page 63.

Games

For fluency work you will need games that encourage the students to use language freely and will also keep all the students interested – even if they can't all join in. So the games will have to go at a good pace and produce some excitement and perhaps suspense.

Organising the class

You have probably noticed that when games are played on TV or radio, there is usually an 'audience'. These are people who have been told the 'answers' and therefore follow the game with interest and amusement. You can use the same device in the classroom too. For example, you can have two teams playing in front of an audience.

TEAM A	AUDIENCE	TEAM B

The students in each team are interested because *they* want to win. The students in the audience are interested because they want to *see* who wins – and how quickly. So everyone in the class is involved.

For some games you can also have a panel of 'experts'. That is, five to six students who have to answer questions or try to find out the answer (depending on the type of game) in front of an audience. You will also need a question master – you or one of the students – who controls the game. In this case most of the class will be listening – but, we hope, with interest.

PANEL

Question master

AUDIENCE

Of course you don't need to have an audience for *every* game. For quick class practice (e.g. about five minutes) just divide the class into two or three teams. The important thing is to keep everybody involved in some way.

Guessing games

Guessing games are very good for class fluency work, especially if you have an audience as suggested above.

For quick practice you can make a lot of use of visual material with plenty of detail. The students have to find out as much as they can about a picture by asking any kind of question. (This is how this activity differs from the one on page 25.) They can make notes or even try to draw the picture as they ask questions. You don't even need to divide them into teams. Here are some other examples of guessing games.

Twenty Questions

The game is called this because the players are allowed to ask up to twenty questions in order to find out the answer. For example:

One or more player thinks of an object, e.g. a bicycle. He gives the other players a 'clue': that is, he tells them something about the object. For example: most of it is metal. The players (the panel, if you have organised the game in this way) then ask a series of *yes/no* questions which, they hope, will lead them to identify the object.

A: Is there one in this room?
B (= *the question master*): No.
C: Do you use this object in the house?
B: No – not usually!
D: So you use it outside .... In the garden?
B: It can be used in the garden. But that's not the usual place.
A: In the street, then?
B: Yes. It's usually used in the road or in the street.
C: And is it heavy?
B: Well, no. Not very. At least not these days. (etc.)

The players continue asking questions in this way until they feel that they know the answer and can ask: *Is it a bicycle*? Remember that, if you have an 'audience' for the game, who already know the answer, they will be following closely.

What's my line?

This and the next two games are like *Twenty Questions*.

One player or more thinks of an occupation (e.g. artist). He can give a clue by miming an action connected with his work. For *artist*, he might pretend to mix some paints or stand back to look at his picture. The other players then ask questions like these: *Do you work alone? Do you work outside? Is your work hard? Do you earn a lot of money?* (etc.)

If you want to make the game a little easier, write a list of jobs on the board which the players have to choose from.

Who am I?

One player pretends to be a famous person. The others try to find out by asking: *Are you (still alive)? Are you (French)? Were you married? (Did) you (write books)?* (etc.)

Where do I live?

One player or more pretends that he comes from a famous city. The others try to find out by asking: *Is it (big)? Is it (an old city)? Is it (near the sea)? Is it in (Europe)?* (etc.)

> ACTIVITY
>
> Think of other guessing games you can play with the whole class.

Memory games

Can you remember the picture?

Show the students a picture with quite a lot of detail in it. Ask them to study the picture for a minute and then turn it round so that they cannot see it. Divide the class into two teams and let them take it in turns to say something about the picture. Give one point for each correct statement (but reward good statements with extra points).

Can you remember the story?

Tell the students a story with quite a lot of detail in it (e.g. dates. physical description, etc.). For example: *It was half past ten on a cold January morning. A tall elderly man was walking down a busy street towards a very large supermarket on the corner. The man – his name was Jack Turner – was wearing a very large black hat, so that it was almost impossible to see his face. Suddenly the man began to ...* Divide the class into two teams and ask them to take it in turns to tell you bits of the story in any order. Give points for correct answers. Then ask students from each team in turn to tell the story sentence by sentence.

Alternatively, after you have told the story, students from each team can take it in turns to question one another about the story. For example: *What time was it? What was the weather like? Where was the supermarket?* (etc.)

> ACTIVITY
>
> Make up a short story with a lot of detail which you could use for the activity above.

Alibi

For this activity the students have to establish that they could not have committed a crime because they were doing something else.

Present the situation. For example: *Two people robbed a bank between 8 and 8.30 last night. The bank was in the High Street.* Ask the students to work in pairs and to agree in as much detail as possible what they were doing from 7 to 9 o'clock. For example, A and B decide: *We went to the cinema at 6 o'clock. Afterwards we went to a cafe at 8.30 and stayed there until 10 o'clock.* They must also think of as many details as they can, e.g. about the cinema, the film, the cafe.

When it is A and B's turn to be questioned, A goes out of the classroom while the other students ask B a lot of questions. For example: *What was the name of the film? Who was in it? How did it end? How long did it last? Was the cinema crowded*? etc. B is then called in and questioned in the same way. If B's answers are different, the students will decide that these two haven't got an alibi. Of course this doesn't prove that they committed the crime ... but it makes an amusing game and the students get really involved in asking searching questions.

Story-telling

Why story-telling is a good classroom activity

Students almost always enjoy listening to stories. They recognise that they belong to 'real life'. And they listen with attention because they want to know how the story goes on and how it ends. Probably, even as you are telling the story, they are trying to work out what happens next!

Although you can and should ask the students to tell stories too, this is one of the things *you* can do without worrying: Am I doing too much talking? Students will listen – provided you tell the story in the right way.

Points to remember

There are two important points to keep in mind:

a) **Don't read the story.**

If you try to read from a text, you will probably 'kill' the story. If you need some help, make an outline of your story in note form – like the one below – which you can easily keep in your head while you are telling the story. But it doesn't matter if you change the story or leave something out. You are the story-teller and the story is what you make it.

b) **Watch the faces of the students.**

It is very important to do this because the expressions on the faces of the students will tell you if they are interested or bored or puzzled. Sometimes you will need to repeat something or say something in a different way. If you watch the students' faces, you will generally be able to tell when this is necessary. Incidentally, you wouldn't be able to do this if you were reading from a text.

Story outlines

Here is an example of a story outline:

Strong man in circus, showing strength.
Broke furniture, bent pieces of metal (etc.)
Each time strong man asked: Anybody like to try to do this?
No one came forward!
Finally, strong man took an orange.
Squeezed it until all the juice ran out.
Again asked: Anybody like to try this?
A weak-looking man came forward. Took
orange and squeezed. Lot of juice came out.
Strong man astonished. Asked: How can you do that?
Weak-looking man answered: I'm a tax collector!

ACTIVITY

Read the outline again and then try to tell the story. Use actions as you tell it to bring the story alive. Change the story as much as you like. For example, think of different things that the strong man could do – which would interest your students.

Where do you find stories?

There are plenty of traditional stories that you can use. But why not make some up for yourself? For example, go back to the story of the man going towards the supermarket on page 67. This story hasn't been written yet! But you can easily think of different ways in which it might continue. Perhaps he began to . . . shout because he saw that the supermarket was on fire. Or run because he saw somebody coming out of the supermarket that he hadn't seen for years. Or perhaps he began to cough because he was very ill . . .

ACTIVITY

Write the rest of this story. Try to make it into something really exciting.

What do the students do?

This is meant to be an enjoyable activity. If the students have enjoyed hearing the story, surely they have 'understood' it – at least enough to give them pleasure? So one thing you mustn't do is test them – through asking questions, for example. Although it is possible that they would like to ask *you* questions.

There are, however, other things you can ask them to do. You can ask them to draw a picture of the people in the story or of some of the events. You can invite them to tell the story in their own words, or to make up a similar story. And as a follow-up activity, you can give the students an outline and ask them to make up their own stories. If you ask them to do this in groups, you will then hear several different versions – all deriving from the same outline.

ACTIVITY

Write outlines for two stories – one original, the other based on a traditional story.

Other skills

Listening

All the activities in this chapter have involved a good deal of listening. It is an essential part of class fluency activities: the students have to listen, either to you or to one another, otherwise they can't take part.
This kind of listening – as part of a game or discussion or story-telling – is really important for the students. That is why you shouldn't worry too much if you find that you are doing a lot of talking (provided this is balanced by pair work and group work activities). If you are talking about something worth listening to, the students will be learning.

Instructions and explanations

Think of the many opportunities you have in the classroom for telling the students what to do or explaining how to do an activity. This is especially true of the fluency activities which the students will do in groups on their own (see Chapter 10). You have to make sure they know what to do before they start, otherwise they will make mistakes or do the activities badly.

In the early stages of the course you will probably have to explain things in the mother tongue – just to be sure that they do know what to do. But, as the course progresses, try not only to explain everything in English, but also conduct the whole lesson without using the mother tongue at all. For the students this is a very *real* use of English. It is like having a job of work explained in a factory or an office.

Listening to recorded materials

So far we have put a lot of emphasis on getting the students to listen to you or to one another. But of course listening to a wide range of recorded materials is also important for developing fluency.

They not only give the students something to talk about, in groups or for whole class work. The students also need to be able to understand much more than they can say and they can only develop this ability if you expose them to all kinds of unedited materials. This kind of exposure is also important for building up confidence – because the students need to get used to *not understanding* everything they hear.

Deductive listening

Usually, when the students listen to recorded materials, you ask them to do a task (e.g. complete a chart with certain bits of information) either while they are listening or immediately afterwards. There is, as we have seen, very little opportunity for immediate interaction.

But there is one way of getting the students to listen *and* talk. You can do this if you present the text (even dialogues in the course-book!) line by line. All you do is pause after each sentence and ask the students to tell you, in as much detail as possible, what they think is happening and what they think is going to happen. Here is an example with a piece of dialogue.

BILL: Ah! You've got a cine-camera.

The students might say: *Bill has just seen the cine-camera. He isn't expecting the other person to have one. He is pleased. Bill probably doesn't know the other person. Also, after seeing the camera, he may ask him to do something ...*

BILL (*going on*): ... Will you make a picture of our village, please?

The students might say: *Right! He does ask the other person to do something for him. Probably the other person will say yes – because it is not such a big thing. Maybe they're going on a visit to Bill's village.*

BUCK: Yes, of course. Why?

The students might say: *Right again! The other person does agree. But he can't think why Bill wants a picture of his village. Bill will almost certainly explain now* (etc.)

As you can see, once the students are used to this technique, it is a very effective way of getting the class to listen, think ... and then talk.

ACTIVITY

The dialogue goes on:

BILL: It's for my friends in Australia.
I want to show them our way of life.

Take each sentence and suggest what sort of things the students might say.

Writing

Most follow-up activities for class fluency work will have to be done in groups (see page 70). But, as for class accuracy work, you can get the students to write to one another in class. But there are some differences.

First, the students have to produce their own texts (i.e. not follow a model, as for accuracy work). Your job is to provide them with a situation. For example:

You are planning to have a party. You want A to come – but you know he doesn't like parties. Try to persuade him to come to yours by making the party sound exciting. Also give some details about the party (place, time, etc.).

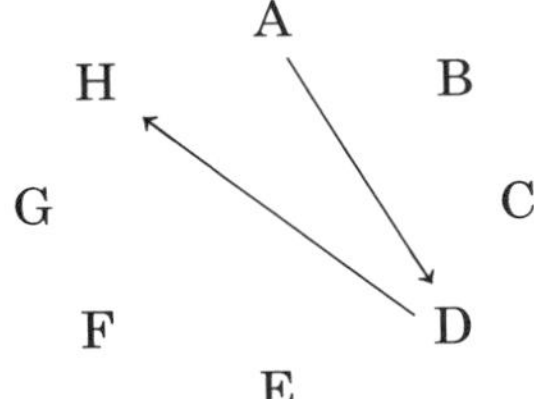

A task along these lines will give the students sufficient guidance.

Secondly, the students must choose or be given a partner to write to. This is partly because the activity will take more time so the students won't be able to write to a lot of people, and partly because he should keep that person in mind while he is writing.

If A writes to D, for example, D must answer A's letter – but D himself will write to somebody else – H, for example.

You can of course give the students simpler tasks than the one above. For example:

Write to a friend in the class. Ask him to go out with you to a café or a cinema after the lesson. Say exactly where to meet.

You can also ask the students to write their letters as homework (keeping in mind the person they are writing to) and then exchange them in class. This makes better use of class time – and homework too!

ACTIVITY

Write more tasks like those above which you could use to get the students to write to one another in the classroom for fluency practice.

Fluency work in groups

Pair work and group work

We can't draw an absolute dividing line between pair work and group work, but there are two important differences:

- size;
- type of activity.

Let's look at each of these in turn.

Size

There is no magic number for groups, but four to eight students in each is a good general guide. Some activities, such as games, work better with a smaller number, because students get a turn more often. If the students have to share ideas, a larger number may be better. But, in the end, it may be the classroom furniture which decides the size of your groups.

For example, if you have tables which are fairly easy to move, get your students to form groups as in the right-hand diagram:

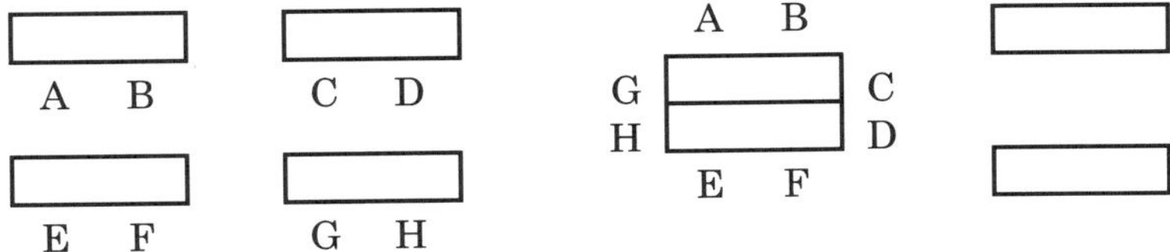

On the other hand, if you have heavy desks that really can't be moved, get the students to work in groups of four like this;

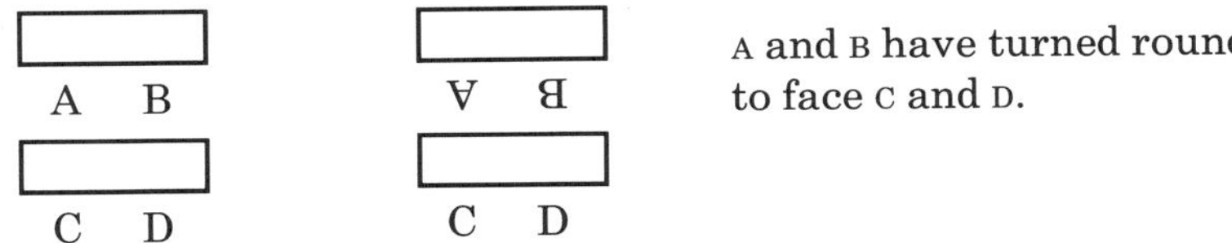

A and B have turned round to face C and D.

The important thing is for the students to be able to work together comfortably.

But don't forget that the more groups you have, the harder it will be for you to keep an eye on them. That is important, too.

Type of activity

You can get the students to do accuracy activities in groups but, unless you can form them quickly, you must ask yourself: Is it worth it? Is it necessary? After all, you may want to do pair work two or three times in a lesson. On the other hand, most fluency activities need the environment of a group and in any case will usually go on for ten to fifteen minutes, perhaps even longer. During this time, the students, working on their own, should sometimes be able to *forget* that they are in a classroom!

Forming groups: mixed or same ability?

On the whole, mixed ability groups – with fast and slow students together – are better for fluency work. (And in any case, if you can't move the students around, you will probably end up with mixed ability groups.) Students *do* help one another, because the kind of work they have to do involves co-operation and collaboration. And you only have to listen in to group work to hear students correcting one another's mistakes!

But won't the slower students hold up the fast ones? Perhaps, to some extent. If you put fast and slow students in separate groups, they can all go at their own pace. So the faster ones will finish the work more quickly or can work at a higher level. But in the end this will create more problems. You will widen the gap between the fast and slow students in the class. And you will also have to find special tasks for each group and prepare each group separately. And you won't be able to share the results with the whole class afterwards – which is an exciting part of group work (see page 79).

If, sometimes, you want to bring the weaker students together so that you can work with them for a while, then simply take these from the 'regular' groups. Otherwise, forming groups on the basis of the same ability is best kept for special circumstances. For example, if you have a class where there is real difference in levels, group work may become an alternative to regular class teaching.

Who controls the groups?

The answer is: the students themselves. Of course you too have a very big responsibility. You must give the students a suitable activity and you must make sure that they know how to do it. But once you have done that, you should get out of the way and let the students get on with it. If they want advice, let them ask for it. Listen in, by all means, but don't interfere. The students must be allowed to feel free, otherwise they won't say what *they* want to say – which is the purpose of fluency work.

But someone must be in charge, surely? So shouldn't each group have a 'leader'? For some activities, it is useful for someone to be in charge and in any case someone has to act as 'reporter' to the class at the end of each session. But the students can take turns to do this.

Why not let the students themselves decide whether they want or need a group leader?

Problems with group work

Let's look here at some of the objections that are sometimes made to group work.

I've got too many students in my class!

But the more students you have, the more necessary group work becomes. Otherwise how can they ever *talk* to one another? But form groups as simply as you can and use simple activities that aren't likely to go wrong.

I can't move the desks in my classroom!

As we have seen, you don't have to! There is always some way in which you can get the students to work together in groups. It doesn't even matter if the groups are all different sizes.

It takes up a lot of time!

It is true that you can easily spend half a lesson – perhaps a whole lesson – on a good group activity. But there are a lot of activities in Chapter 10 which can be done in ten to fifteen minutes. Of course you won't be able to do group work every lesson. But try to do some group work once a week – so that the students really get a chance to use what they have learnt.

The students won't talk in English!

Of course the students will sometimes start to use their mother tongue to express an idea – especially if they get excited. But this is natural if they want to communicate. However, it is part of your job to see that activities are roughly at the right level and also that the students learn how to make the best use of the little they know. You can often show them that during class fluency work.

The best students will do all the work!

Certainly some students may be lazy. And it can also happen that one or two students force their ideas on the rest of the group. But in general, most students work harder in groups because they are more involved. They are also quite able to see that everyone contributes. If you think that something is seriously wrong, join the group for a while and try to sort the problem out.

The students will make mistakes and I won't be able to correct them!

It is true that they will make more mistakes than they did for accuracy practice. They will make mistakes because they are trying to express their own ideas. But look at the positive side, too. First, the students aren't making mistakes all the time. They are using quite a lot of correct language too. Secondly, they do correct one another. It isn't in fact your job to try to correct mistakes.

How do I know if my students are learning anything?

You can't of course measure their 'progress' as you can when the students are learning grammar and vocabulary. But you can tell how well they are doing from the way they do the activities and the language they use. Using language in this way is an essential part of *learning*.

Group work: points to keep in mind

Form the groups in the simplest way possible.

Don't move desks more than necessary. Try to get four to eight students in each group.

Have mixed ability groups.

This should be the normal practice unless you have a special reason for separating fast from slow students.

Select the activities for group work carefully.

Of course you want activities that will encourage the students to use English freely and also make the best use of what they know.

But there is no point in giving them activities which will frustrate them because they haven't got the language to do them adequately.

Present the activities carefully.

Make sure that the students know exactly what to do before they divide into groups.

Don't interfere with group work unless something is seriously wrong.

Let the students take responsibility for what they are doing. If they haven't understood something, you can stop them, explain and get them to start again.

Don't correct mistakes.

Make a note of anything serious and reteach it in another lesson.

Stop group work at an appropriate moment.

That is, at the end of the time you have given the students. As for pair work, you mustn't let activities drag on, with some students getting bored.

Show results.

Get the groups to report to one another what they have done (this is another fluency activity). In general, follow this pattern of work:

PRESENT AND EXPLAIN ACTIVITIES (Class) → ACTIVITIES (Groups) → REPORT RESULTS AND DISCUSSION (Class)

Examples of fluency work in groups

Discussion

As for class work, discussion means 'talk' (see page 59). The examples in this section are arranged in categories, according to the main idea, but they often overlap.

Interpretation activities

For these the students have to decide what they *think* something means. Some ways of doing this are through:

Pictures

Every picture tells a story – but usually more than one! Look at the picture below. What do *you* think it is about?

The two people in the picture are probably in a park ... but who are they? Are they husband and wife, friends ... or two people who don't know one another – yet? They look annoyed, but are they annoyed with one another or with someone else? And what are they annoyed about? And what will happen after this? When *you* were deciding what this situation was about, you probably answered all these questions without thinking about it!

This is clearly a good way of getting students to talk. First of all, they can all give their ideas and argue with one another. And then they can be asked to try to agree, as a group, on one interpretation. That is, to make up some sort of story about the picture.

The two discussion stages

While they are talking about the picture, they will probably say things like this (though of course they will make mistakes):

A (*who is giving his ideas*): Well, *I* think she's angry with the man.
B: Why? What happened?
A: Well, he's her husband. And he promised to meet her in the park.
C: When?
A: Oh, one afternoon. At four o'clock. But he was late.
B: Why?
A: Well, he was walking along the street and he met a friend. And they talked a lot.
D: What about?
A: Oh, ...
C: Football!
B: Politics!
D: I think he went to a cafe with his friend ...
A: Well, he was late. His wife shouted at him because she was waiting for a long time. And after that ... (etc.)

The students will probably discuss two or three interpretations like this. In fact, this is the most important part of the discussion. But you want them to have something to tell the class afterwards, so ask them also to work out one version – or perhaps accept the one they like the best. Let's imagine that the group likes A's interpretation. The story they tell the other groups will be something like this:

> One afternoon Mr and Mrs White decided to meet in the park at four o'clock. Mrs White came to the park on time. But her husband was late because he met a friend in the street and they

began to talk. Mrs White sat there, getting angrier and angrier. And when her husband came, she started shouting and he started shouting. Then they sat without talking and finally it began to rain, so they went home.

> ACTIVITY
>
> Work out at least three more possible interpretations for the picture.

Dialogue work

Pictures of this kind will often lead on naturally to dialogue activities. For example, for the picture above, what did the two people say to one another? The group we have been looking at could produce the following dialogue between Mr and Mrs White – which they can act out or give to another group to act out.

MRS W: Where have you been? It's half past four!
MR W: It can't be! (*Looks at watch.*)
Oh, my watch is slow!
MRS W: What an excuse! I don't believe you.
I came here on time. Why can't *you*?
I think you met someone!
MR W: I didn't! You never believe me!
MRS W: Because you never tell the truth! (etc.)

Types of picture

You can use almost any kind of picture for this activity (even some of those in the coursebook), but try to find some that will encourage a lot of different ideas. These can be very simple, like the one below – which you could draw on the board.

ACTIVITY

Work out two or three possible interpretations for this picture.

Pictures of faces

You will find pictures of faces especially useful. You can ask the students to decide about the person's:

- age
- nationality
- marital status (if married, single, divorced)
- education
- occupation
- hobbies
- personality

In short, get them to work out a short biography.

ACTIVITY

What would you say about these people? Notice the language you use in talking or writing about them.

Here are other suggestions for interpretation activities. They won't all produce so much discussion as pictures but they will get the students talking. Notice that some of them, such as speech bubbles and newspaper headlines, don't require any materials. You can just write them on the board.

Single object pictures

You can use (once again) the picture sheet on page 43. Give the students a situation. For example:

> A woman found the bike outside her front door when she opened it one morning.
>
> A man went to work with a very large pair of scissors in his bag.

Ask them to make up a story around these situations.

Strange stories

Ask the students to explain strange situations like these:

> They went into the room. It was full of cardboard boxes. There were hundreds of them, all different sizes. They were all empty except for one small box near the window. This had a sandwich in it.

Short dialogues

The students have to say who is speaking, where they are and what they are talking about. For example:

A: It's nice here, isn't it?
B: Mm. Do you come here often?
A: Not so much as I used to. I can't always get away these days.

Speech bubbles

For example:

If you do that again, I'll.....!

For these you can:

- give the students the place (house, office, street . . .) and ask them to say who is speaking and about what;
- give the students several places and ask them to suggest a different interpretation for each;
- ask the students to decide on the place as well.

Sounds

For example, the students listen to the following sequences and decide what is happening.

> telephone rings – footsteps – door closes
>
> wind blowing – voices – rocks falling – dog barking – wind blowing

Remember that sounds are not permanent. The students will need to hear the sequences two or three times, discuss what they are (as a class) and perhaps make a note of what they have heard.

Headlines

For example:

The students have to make up a story to fit the headlines. Book titles can be used in the same way. For example: *Across the Sahara on a Bicycle. When I Was Young.*

Doodles

That is, the sort of drawings people make just to pass the time. For example:

The students can draw these for one another.

> ACTIVITY
>
> Write more short dialogues, strange stories, speech bubbles and headlines.

Problem-solving activities

These activities present the students with some kind of problem which they have to solve. There isn't, however, just one 'solution' – so this results in a lot of talk.

'Survival' situations

The 'problem' the students face here is how to stay alive – or at least live as comfortably as possible!

Desert Island

Tell the students: You are going to spend the next (three) months on an island – alone. There is fresh water and vegetation, and no real danger from wild animals. Choose (five) of the following objects to take with you and put them in order of importance. Be prepared to say why you want to take these things.

Give the students a list of objects. For example:

axe	***hammer***	***paper and pencil***
blanket	***knife***	***rope***
clock	***ladder***	***saucepan***
gun	***matches***	***telescope***
guitar	***medicine box***	***trumpet***

You can write this list on the board and you can allow the students one free choice. That is, they can take one object which *isn't* on the list. Notice that once again you could use a picture sheet like the one on page 43 for this activity.

The students then choose their objects individually (or, work in pairs within the group so that there is talk at this stage too) and also think of their reasons. They then compare their lists. This clearly produces a lot of talk and the activity could stop at this point (that is, without a class follow-up).

But you can also ask each group to produce a list of objects on which they all agree, which they then compare with other groups.

Some variations on Desert Island

Here are some ways of adapting the activity so that the students will still be interested if you ask them to repeat it.

- Each student in turn chooses one object from the list (and gives his reasons, etc.). No one else is allowed to have this object, so the next student has to choose a different object each time (whether or not he would have liked to take the same object).
- The students have to choose (five) objects which they could use if they were trying to escape from the island. They must say how they would use them.

You can also use different survival situations. For example: how to survive for three weeks in the desert, in a boat at sea, on top of a mountain – or on the moon. Each situation will need a different list of objects.

> ACTIVITY
>
> Prepare a list of objects for each of the situations above. You can include some 'fun' items too.

You can also ask the students to compile their own list of objects for any of these situations. This again will produce quite a lot of talk.

Finally, as a fun activity, tell the students that they are going to the moon – and not coming back to earth again. Ask them to make a list of (ten) objects they would like to take with them as souvenirs of their life here.

> ACTIVITY
>
> Make a list of other 'survival' situations which you could use with a class.

Finding differences and similarities

For a version of this in the form of a game, see page 94. For a group discussion activity, give each group a pair of similar pictures (e.g. two rooms, streets, maps, etc.) and ask them to make a list of the differences and similarities.

If you haven't got duplicate sets of the pictures, ask each group in turn to work with a pair of pictures, then exchange these with another group. In this way at least two groups will be able to compare their ideas.

Instead of pictures, you can give the students pairs of words. For example, *places* (cinema/theatre); *jobs* (doctor/dentist); *animals* (horse/elephant), etc. Here is an example of what the students might write about horses and elephants.

Differences	***Similarities***
1 Elephants have trunks	***1 They don't eat meat***
2 Horses have big tails	***2 They both work***
3 Elephants don't have hair	***3 People ride on them***

ACTIVITY

Make a list of ten other pairs of words for this activity.

Forming groups

Give the students a list of words (e.g. animals) and ask them to divide them into two groups according to whether, for example, they are dangerous/not dangerous; domestic/wild; big/small; meat-eaters/not meat-eaters, etc.

You can also ask the students to find their own groups for lists of words.

Some possible areas and groups are:

jobs: actor, baker, dentist ... (indoor/outdoors; with people/alone; interesting/boring, etc.)

everyday objects: basket, lamp, spoon, umbrella ... (useful/not very useful; cheap/expensive; used indoors/used outside, etc.)

transport: boat, car, train ... (old/modern; noisy/quiet; slow/fast, etc.)

people: Napoleon, Gandhi, Shakespeare, Cleopatra, Princess Diana ... (alive/dead; male/female; artistic/not artistic; good-looking/not good-looking, etc.)

ACTIVITIES

1 Complete the lists above so that you have about fifteen items in each and work out more possible groups.

2 Make a list of other areas you could use for this activity: e.g. food, cities, ...

Grading

The students have to put items in order of preference, importance, size, etc. Here is an example of a task.

> ***Arrange these animals in order from most dangerous to least dangerous.***
>
> | | | | |
> |---|---|---|---|
> | ***bear*** | ***goat*** | ***kangaroo*** | ***tiger*** |
> | ***cat*** | ***giraffe*** | ***lion*** | ***sheep*** |
> | ***dog*** | ***gorilla*** | ***elephant*** | ***zebra*** |

You can also ask the students to grade these animals according to how strong, fast, clever, common, attractive, etc. they are.

Some other possible areas are:

pets: interesting, common, easy to look after, ...
food: healthy, cheap, pleasant to eat, ...
people: famous, clever, good, ...
materials: useful, expensive, common, ...
sports: fun, dangerous, cheap, ...

> ACTIVITIES
>
> 1 Find more ways of grading the items above.
>
> 2 Find five more areas which you could use for this activity.

Deciding on qualities

The students have to decide what qualities they would expect to find in, for example, a friend, or put a list of qualities in order. For example:

> ***When you choose a friend, which of these qualities are important?***
>
> ***amusing, attractive, generous, good-tempered,***
>
> ***helpful, intelligent, similar interests,***

You can also ask the students to decide on or put in order the qualities they would look for in: a husband, wife, boy-friend, girl-friend, doctor, politician, bank manager, tenant, teacher.

> ACTIVITY
>
> List ten qualities for each of the words above.

Working out consequences

The students have to discuss and decide what they think would happen if, for example, there was no paper left in the world. (*There wouldn't be any newspapers ... People would telephone more ... We wouldn't have to do homework*! etc.)

Other possible topics are:

- ... if we didn't need to eat?
- ... if we could walk on water?
- ... if we didn't need to sleep?

> ACTIVITY
>
> Make a list of more topics which you could use for this activity.

Planning activities

These activities get the students to talk in order to make certain decisions. Most of them are quite simple and do not require a lot of explanation or extra materials.

Planning a park

See page 62, where this activity was presented as a simulation. Using the same situation, you can ask the students to decide what they want to have in their park and also exactly how they want it to look. They must draw a detailed plan for this, like the one below.

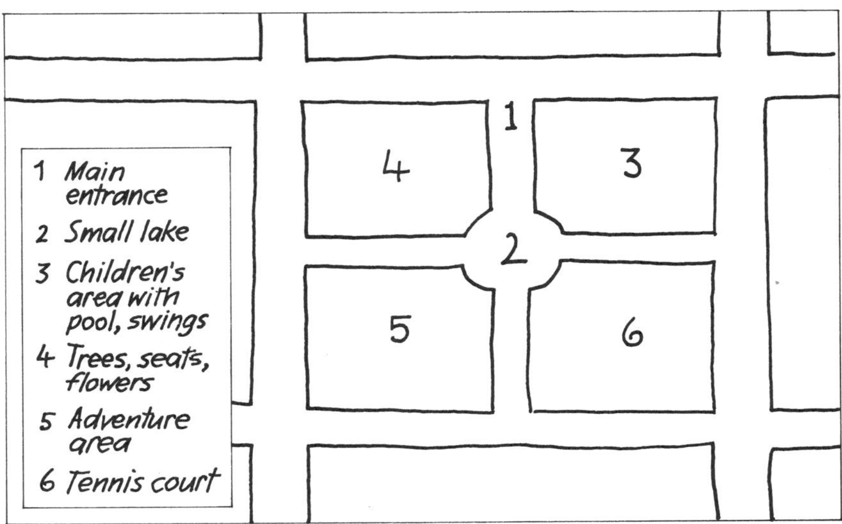

Afterwards the groups can compare their plans, but this kind of material should also be displayed if possible.

Planning a club

This is similar to planning a park. Draw a plan of a building on the board and tell the students that it is available as a social club. Ask them to suggest some of the facilities they would like their club to have: for example, snack bar, disco, library. The groups then have to work out their own final list of facilities and decide where to place them in the building.

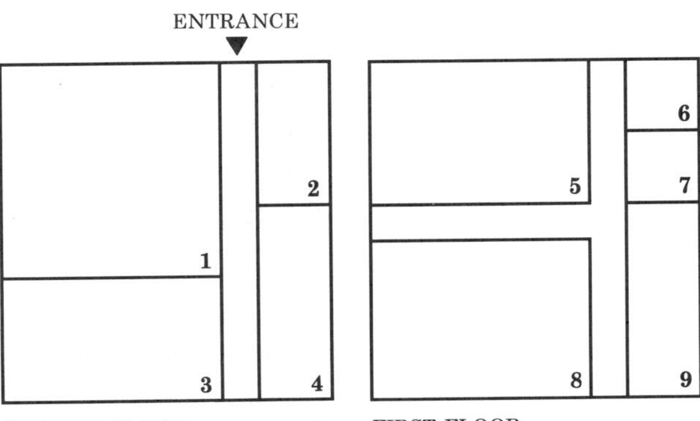

Here are some suggestions for other planning activities:

- *a picnic*: where to go, how to go, what to eat and drink, what other things to take, what to do on the picnic;
- *a visit to a city*: where to go, what to see and in what order, what to do if it rains;
- *a guided tour of the students' own town for a foreign visitor*: what to see and in what order, where to eat;
- *a zoo*: which animals to have and where to put them in the zoo (so that they do not annoy one another, the zoo is interesting for visitors).

The students can also be asked to plan campaigns: e.g. to stop people smoking, to improve the facilities in their town, to raise money for old people (disasters, etc.).

Planning activities of this kind obviously have a lot of educational value too, and you may want to turn them into projects (see page 101).

ACTIVITY

Make a list of five more planning activities like those above.

Invention activities

The main purpose of these it is get the students to use their imaginations in order to talk (and to some extent they are similar to *interpretation activities*).

For example, you can ask the students to:

- invent connections between two objects: e.g. jacket – glass. This can be in the form of a short story.
- invent uses for an object: e.g. an empty tin can.
- invent machines: e.g. for making rain, making money, doing homework, etc.

One simple but effective way of getting the students to exercise their imaginations is to draw a window on the board and to ask them to imagine what the room on the other side is like; who is in it and what they are doing. You can also draw a wall on the board and ask the students to imagine what is on the other side.

> ACTIVITY
>
> Suggest other invention activities.

Games

All the games which were used for class fluency work can be played in groups (with the exception of *Alibi*). The following games are particularly suitable for group work.

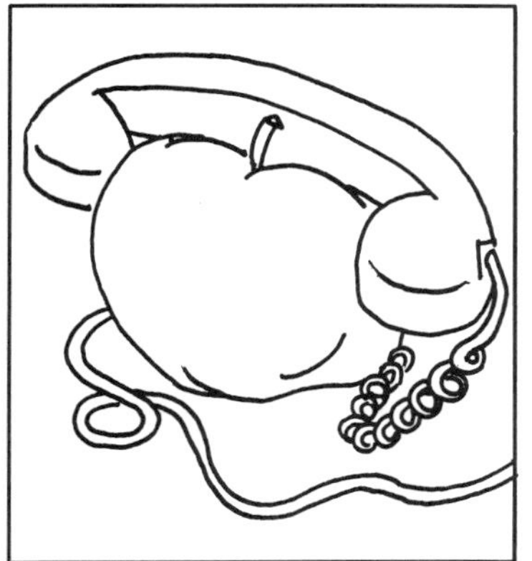

Describe and draw

One player, A, has a picture which the others in the group are not allowed to see. A has to describe the picture so that the others can draw it as exactly as possible. They can ask for more information while they are doing this – and they must, of course, listen to one another's questions. More than one player can share the job of describing the picture. For example:

	B
A	C
	D

	C
A	
	D
B	
	E

A	D
B	E
C	F

Instead of drawing the picture immediately, the students who are listening can make notes and then use these notes afterwards to draw the picture, either individually or together.

Finally the students who have drawn the picture(s) compare their version(s) with the original and discuss any differences.

> ACTIVITIES
>
> 1 Work out the description that A will need to give for the picture above.
>
> 2 Find or draw five more pictures for this activity.

Find the difference

See page 46 for a pair work version of this activity. There the students drew their own pictures and tried to find out the differences using very controlled language. For fluency work the students have no idea how their pictures are different and therefore have to ask all sorts of questions to find out what the differences are. If the differences are very small, as in the pictures below, the students will have to talk a lot in order to find, say, five differences. You can ask the students to find out as many differences as possible in (five) minutes or to find out a set number of differences.

ACTIVITIES

1 Find the differences between the two pictures above and try to work out the kind of language the students will use when they are talking.

2 Find more pairs of pictures suitable for this activity. You can try drawing simple pictures or maps.

Complete it

For this activity you need picture sequences that tell a story (for example, like the one on page 100). Each player or pair of players has one picture and therefore knows part of the story. They try to work out the story by exchanging information – first trying to get the pictures in order and then working out the details of the story.

See page 103 for a reading activity along the same lines.

Use it

For the three games above the students have been *exchanging information*: that is, telling one another certain things in order to complete a task. For *Use it*, the students exchange opinions – so it is much more like a discussion game.

Each group of players has two sets of small object cards like those in the picture set on page 43.

Set 1 'Occupation' cards (one for each player in the group). The objects on these cards represent occupations. So if A, for example, gets a picture of a *ladder*, he can decide to be a builder, a window cleaner . . . or even a burglar!

Set 2 This consists of about twenty to twenty-five object cards which the students have to use in the course of the game.

The game is played like this. Both sets of cards are placed face downwards on the table. Each student takes an occupation card, chooses an occupation and tells the others what it is. Each student in turn then picks up an object card and says how he would use it in his work. For example, if A is a window cleaner and he picks up a picture of a saucepan, he can say he will use it for carrying water to clean the windows. If the other students like what he says – and there should be some discussion – A can keep the card. If not, he must put the card back on the table. The game goes on until all the cards have been used.

Board games

You can use the board game on page 43 – with its many variations – for fluency work too. Just encourage the students to use language freely – and to talk while they are playing, as if they were playing a game *outside* the classroom.

However, here is an idea for a board game which you can use specially for fluency work.

Ask the students to make their own boards, like this one:

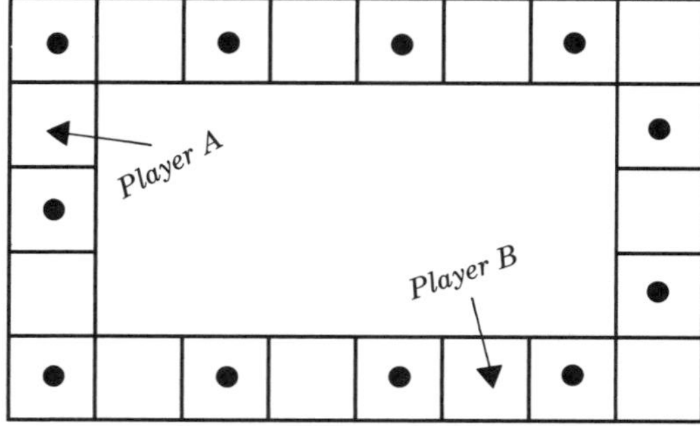

The board consists of a continuous track, divided into squares. There should be at least twenty-five to thirty squares, but the exact number is not important. There are dots or circles on alternate squares. When they play, the students can start on *any* square they like, except one that has a dot or circle on it. These are 'penalty' squares. If they land on one of these during the game, they have to do something.

The players throw a dice to move and they go round the board clockwise. Player A, for example, throws a 4. He lands on a blank square, so he doesn't have to do anything. But Player B throws a 1, so he lands on a square with a circle on it. He has to do the first task on the list.

1 Sing a song.

2 Persuade the person on your right to buy you a coffee.

3 Name six illnesses.

4 Walk round the room backwards.

5 Draw a picture of your face.

The players have to take the tasks in order.

For another version of the game, give the players a list of objects (or get them to write their own). For example:

an axe	***a large mirror***
a cake	***a child's doll***
a camera	***a carpet***

Then explain the situation: while you are walking down the street at three o'clock in the morning, with (an axe) in your hand, you meet a policeman. He stops you – and asks what you are doing with it. You must give him a good reason! Depending how much the other players like your excuse, you get 1–3 points.

The player with the most points at the end of the game (e.g. after (five) minutes – because there is no real end to the game) is the winner. In fact the 'winner' for this game is not important. What matters is to make up good excuses!

ACTIVITIES

1 Write fifteen more tasks for each version of the game above.
2 Suggest other situations for the second version of the game.

Role play

Before you read this section, have another look at role play activities in Chapter 6. Role play is explained there and there are also examples of controlled activities. In fact, controlling the language of these activities is very difficult because students naturally want to speak for themselves. This makes role play especially suitable for fluency work. So you can use some of the activities in Chapter 6 for fluency work too, particularly the menu on page 40 and the TV programmes on page 41.

But remember that some students, especially adolescents, don't find it easy to pretend to be someone else – even if they are only doing this in front of other students within the group. Luckily this doesn't matter too much because role play involves other things too. Look at the stages below:

a) The students discuss the activity. That is, they read their instructions and work out what they have to do. (They may sometimes have to do this in their mother tongue).

b) They work out what they will say. They may decide to change the situation so that there are more speakers. They can also discuss the scene too – where the action takes place. Notice that all the students can contribute here – even the shy ones!

c) They practise the role play within the group – with or without you listening. Again, most students will be ready to take part, at least after a time.

d) They decide how they will – or could – present their role play in front of the class. This is an optional stage, but even if they don't do the role play in front of the other students, they can still discuss where they will stand and what 'props' (tables, chairs, bags, etc.) they will need.

e) They present their activity.

Although the last stage is optional, it is a little like the final stage of a discussion activity, where the students compare their ideas across the class. Give the students the chance, therefore, to show what they have done to the rest of the class, but don't compel them to do it if they don't want to.

Here are some suggestions for role play activities for fluency work.

Incomplete dialogues

Give the students the beginning of a conversation and ask them to continue it for themselves. For example:

A Travel agent

B Customer

A: Good morning. Can I help you?

B: Well, I'm looking for a cheap holiday!

A: A cheap holiday? Well, let's see . . .
What sort of holiday are you thinking of?
I mean, where and for how long? . . . .

Usually the students find it easy to develop a situation like this. But you must stress that it isn't enough just to work out what these two people say. They must also discuss who they are and what the office is like, etc. They can also bring in more people: e.g. two people who want a holiday, a telephone call for the travel agent.

> ACTIVITIES
>
> 1 Suggest two or three ways of developing the role play above.
>
> 2 Write an incomplete dialogue for another role play situation.

Role instructions

For the situation above, for example, these could be as follows:

> ***You and a friend want to go on holiday together. Decide what sort of holiday you would like (e.g. where, when, how long for, how much you can pay, etc.). Talk to the travel agent and see if he has a holiday for you.***

If you cannot give the groups any holiday information (e.g. old travel brochures), ask half the students to act as travel agents, working out details of special cheap holidays, and the other half to discuss some holidays they would like. The group then comes together for the second stage of the activity.

> ACTIVITY
>
> Work out some role instructions to be used together with the menu on page 40 and the TV programmes on page 41.

Scenarios

These are like stories: they describe what happens – but they do not include any dialogue.

You can use a picture sequence for this activity (e.g. picture compositions).

Or you can give the students a text:

> Some people decided to have a picnic. They found a nice place and put out all their food and drink. They were just about to eat when they saw a bear watching them. They got up as quickly as they could and ran off to a safe place. The bear sat down and ate all the food – while the people watched. The bear got up and walked off. The people came back – but there was nothing for them to eat, so they packed up their things and went home.

Scenarios give the students plenty to talk about. But they have to decide for themselves when the people in the story speak and what they say – as well as changing the story to suit themselves (perhaps there are *two* bears . . . who talk while they are eating!). Scenarios are more relaxed than other forms of role play, so they can be a good way of introducing the students to this activity.

ACTIVITIES

1 Decide where the people in the scenario above speak and what they say.

2 Write another scenario.

Project work

Project work involves some kind of *research* (reading, interviewing, etc.) and the production of some kind of *document* (a report, a wall-sheet, a magazine, etc.). It also involves a lot of *discussion*, which is what makes it important for fluency work. However, it can take up a lot of time, so you will have to decide carefully what kind of project work you are going to give the students.

You can turn some of the planning activities (see page 90) into small projects. For example, planning a park. The students will have to read about parks (perhaps in the mother tongue); find out how much facilities cost (which may involve visits to local offices and shops) and interview people about the kind of facilities they would like a park to have.

All this is educationally valuable but, if it isn't possible to send the students out of school for a morning or an afternoon, perhaps the best alternative is to enrich the planning activity by giving them, for example, some background reading on parks and by getting them to role play some interviews in the classroom. You can use the role play cards on page 62 for this.

ACTIVITY

Which of the planning activities on pages 90–2 could be used for project work? How would you adapt them?

A class magazine

One popular form of project work is to get the students to produce a class magazine once a term or once a year. This is a good way of providing a focus for a lot of writing activities during the year. If possible, try to take the students on at least one outside visit to a magazine office, where they can talk to people who actually do this kind of work. If you can't do this, talk to the students about newspaper/magazine offices and get them to do some reading. Also get them to look at magazines to see what they contain and how they are organised.

After that, follow these stages:

a) CLASS Decide on contents of the magazine (e.g. stories, cartoons, jokes, puzzles, features, etc.). Divide these among the groups.

b) GROUPS Select material (any students from the class can send in material) or write it.

c) CLASS Discussion of material. Allocate pages to the groups.

d) GROUPS Organise the material on each page. Edit material if necessary.

e) CLASS Produce the magazine. The students will have to work together (e.g. doing jobs such as typing, checking material, etc.) but not in their original groups.

> ACTIVITY
>
> Make a list of the kind of material which students could produce for a magazine of this kind.

Other skills

Group work provides almost constant opportunities for integrating skills because the students *have* to talk when they are doing a reading or writing activity – and they *have* to listen to one another all the time.

Listening

No special activities are suggested for this but the students can:

- collaborate on tasks related to listening activities. This gets them to discuss what they heard – or what they *think* they heard.
- do the activities described in Chapter 4 pages 25–28. There they were accuracy activities, but when the students do them on their own, they become a test of fluency.

Reading

In addition to collaborating on reading tasks (see Chapter 6 page 51), the students can:

- put in order jumbled sentences to make a paragraph or jumbled paragraphs to make a longer text. The students can do this in the form of a game. See *Complete it* on page 94. Instead of a picture, each student or pair of students has a piece of text.
- interpret instructions for drawing a map or a picture. See the writing activities below.
- compare opinions about a topic. For example, each student or pair of students has a text. The ones below are about plans to open a supermarket.

I think it's a bad idea. It will cause traffic problems and besides, we don't need one – we've got lots of small shops....

It's a really fantastic idea! We'll be able to do all our shopping in one place. It'll be quicker and a lot cheaper too!...

The students compare and discuss opinions, decide who agrees with who and whether they would support a supermarket, etc.

> ACTIVITY
>
> Find or write texts which could be used for the first and last activities above. For the last activity, you can continue writing the texts for and against the supermarket.

Writing

Collaborating on writing activities is one of the most fruitful aspects of group work. It helps the students to see writing as a *useful* activity. For example, they have to make notes or write up an activity (their interpretation of pictures, for example, and the conversations they are going to use for role play). But, perhaps best of all, there is the material which they can write for other groups to *use*. For example, students can work together to write:

- questions on a text, which they then exchange with another group;
- quizzes, which they pass on to be read and answered;
- questionnaires, which they then use for interviewing individually;
- scenarios, which are then used by another group for role play. Students see their own work performed!
- reading material, such as comparing opinions above. The students can also write jumbled stories. That is, they write two short stories (four to five sentences each) and then mix them up to make one story.
- instructions or tasks for a game. For example, they can write for another group the tasks for the board game on page 96. These can take different forms. For example:

> ***If the student on your right is older than you, go back six squares.***
>
> ***If you are wearing jeans, go forward two squares.***

- instructions for drawing a picture or a map. For this the students have to draw a picture, like the one below, noting down step by step what they have done.

They then write out the instructions. For example:

First, draw two chairs. One is on the left and one is on the right. They are facing one another. Next, draw a long piece of wood. It is lying on the two chairs. It is quite strong!
Now draw a man. He is standing on the piece of wood.

Notice that this is not an easy activity. The students may have to write their instructions several times before they can be sure that they are exact.

ACTIVITIES

1 Complete the instructions for drawing the picture above.

2 Draw a picture of your own and write out the instructions for drawing it. Give it to a friend to draw!

Summary of activities

TEACHER CONTROLLED

WHOLE CLASS ACTIVITIES

ACCURACY ←→ FLUENCY

A Drills Games Controlled conversation Listening Writing	C Conversation Discussion Simulation Games Story-telling Listening Writing
B Exercises Controlled conversation Role play Games Questionnaires Listening Writing	D Discussion Games Role play Project work Listening Reading Writing

PAIR WORK ←——→ GROUP WORK

LEARNER DIRECTED

Index of activities

Suggestions for further reading

Books

BYRNE, D *Teaching Oral English* (New Edition) (Longman 1986)
HOLDEN, S (ed.) *Visual Aids for Classroom Interaction* (Modern English Publications 1978)
HOLDEN, S (ed.) *Second Selections from Modern English Teacher* (Longman 1983)
HUBBARD, P, JONES, H, THORNTON, B and WHEELER, R *A Training Course for TEFL* (Oxford University Press 1983)
MATTHEWS, A, DANGERFIELD, L and SPRATT, M (eds.) *At the Chalkface* (Arnold 1985)
RIXON, S *How to Use Games in Language Teaching* (Macmillan 1981)
UR, P *Discussions that Work* (Cambridge University Press 1984)
WINN-BELL OLSEN, J *Communication Starters* (Pergamon 1982)
WRIGHT, A, BETTERIDGE, D and BUCKBY, M *Games for Language Learning* (Cambridge University Press 1984)

Journals

Modern English Teacher (Modern English Publications)
Practical English Teacher (Mary Glasgow Baker)